*Save the World on Your Own Time*

# Save the World
## ON YOUR OWN TIME

# Stanley Fish

**OXFORD**
UNIVERSITY PRESS

# OXFORD
## UNIVERSITY PRESS

Oxford University Press, Inc., publishes works that further
Oxford University's objective of excellence
in research, scholarship, and education.

Oxford  New York
Auckland  Cape Town  Dar es Salaam  Hong Kong  Karachi
Kuala Lumpur  Madrid  Melbourne  Mexico City  Nairobi
New Delhi  Shanghai  Taipei  Toronto

With offices in
Argentina  Austria  Brazil  Chile  Czech Republic  France  Greece
Guatemala  Hungary  Italy  Japan  Poland  Portugal  Singapore
South Korea  Switzerland  Thailand  Turkey  Ukraine  Vietnam

Published by Oxford University Press, Inc.
198 Madison Avenue, New York, New York 10016
www.oup.com

First issued as an Oxford University Press paperback, 2012

Oxford is a registered trademark of Oxford University Press

Previous versions of certain portions of this book appeared in
different form in *Change, Harper's Magazine*, the *Chicago Tribune*,
the *Chronicle of Higher Education*, and the *New York Times*.

Library of Congress Cataloging-in-Publication Data
Fish, Stanley Eugene.
Save the world on your own time / Stanley Fish.
p. cm.
Includes bibliographical references and index.
ISBN 978-0-19-536902-1 (hardcover); 978-0-19-989297-6 (paperback)
1. College teachers—United States—Political activity.
2. Education, Higher—Aims and objectives—United States.
3. Education, Higher—Political aspects—United States.   I. Title.
LB2331.72.F57 2008
378.1'2—dc22      2008008146

1  3  5  7  9  8  6  4  2

Printed in the United States of America
on acid-free paper

*To the memory of my mother,*
*Ida Fish*

# Acknowledgments

My greatest debt is to Cybele Tom of Oxford University Press, who received a medley of disparate essays—some too long, some too short, all too repetitive—and in a remarkably short time transformed an unformed mass into something that actually had a shape. The work of revising and refining that shape took a bit more time, but it would not have been possible were it not for Cybele's initial creative act. I am grateful to my agent Melissa Flashman for finding Cybele and for believing in a project that others sometimes doubted. Without the help of Mary Olszewska, who organized my life and kept track of all its loose ends, none of this would have been put together in the first place. These three did the work so that I could get the credit. Thank you.

# Contents

*Save the World on Your Own Time*

# Introduction

Not long ago, there was a time when I was responsible for a college with close to 30 departments and units, a budget of between 50 and 55 million dollars, 400 tenure-track faculty members, 700 staff, 10,000 undergraduate students, 2,000 graduate students, and 17 buildings. On any given day, I had to deal with disciplinary proceedings, tenure and promotion cases, faculty searches, chair searches, enrollment problems, fundraising, community outreach, alumni relations, public relations, curriculum reform, counteroffers, technology failures, space allocation, information systems, chair meetings, advisory committee meetings, deans council meetings, meetings with the provost, student complaints, faculty complaints, parent complaints, and taxpayer complaints. Office hours were 8:30 a.m. to whenever and often extended into the evenings and weekends. Vacations were few and far between. The pressure never relaxed.

When I left the job after slightly more than five years, I felt that I had all the time (well, not quite all) in the world at my disposal, and for a while, spent it by trying to improve everyone I met, whether or not those I ministered to welcomed my efforts.

I took my opportunities wherever I found them. While I still lived in Chicago, but after I stepped down as dean, the building next door to mine was bought by a developer. For a long time, no development occurred, and the lawn and bushes were allowed to grow wild. The developer, however, had made the mistake of putting his telephone number on an overlarge sign, and as a reward he received a series of dyspeptic phone calls from me accusing him of being a bad neighbor, an irresponsible landlord, and an all-around no-goodnik.

During the same period, I would go into a store or stand in a ticket line and was often greeted by someone who asked, "And how are you today, young man?" That is my least-favorite salutation, and I quickly delivered a lecture and, I trust, a bit of improvement: "When you call someone who is obviously not young 'young man,' what you are doing is calling attention to his age and making him feel even older than he is; don't do it again!"

I delivered an even longer lecture to the blameless fast-food workers who routinely handed me a bagel along with a small container of cream cheese and a plastic knife that couldn't cut butter. I said, "Look, if I wanted to put my own bagel together, I would have bought the ingredients and taken them home; when I go to a restaurant I expect service; I don't expect to be asked to do your job; and besides there's not enough cream cheese here to cover the bagel's surface; what's the matter with you guys?"

But those were just my weekend activities. Although I was no longer a dean, I couldn't shake the habit of being at the office every day, all day. Because I had nothing particular to do, I roamed the halls looking for things that were wrong, and I found them.

Stray pieces of furniture you couldn't give away sat (or sprawled) in front of an office door. I stuck my head in and informed the occupant (why did he or she listen to me?) that the offending items must be removed by the end of the day.

Continuing down the halls, I found the panels separating two elevators festooned with announcements of lectures that took place two years ago. I proceeded to rip the leaflets down. Halfway through I decided that no one should be posting anything there anyway; so I removed every announcement, no matter how current, and, for good measure, I tore away the surface the announcements adhered to and threw all the thumbtacks and push-pins into the trash.

I noticed that someone had left a small carton of books, intended no doubt for impecunious graduate students who might have made good use of them. I didn't care; into the trash they went, too.

Next, I went into the new cafe in the main administration building and saw that the rug on the floor was full of crumbs and looked as if it hadn't been vacuumed in days. No one knew whose job it was, and I took it as my job to find out. I returned to my office and made phone calls until I found someone who answered her phone, although in a short time she wished she hadn't.

But then it was time to go to class (I was still teaching), where, in an enclosed space, my students received the full force of my reforming zeal. I told them that I hadn't the slightest interest in whatever opinions they might have and didn't want to hear any. I told them that while they may have been taught that the purpose of writing is to express oneself, the selves they had were not worth expressing, and that it would be good if they actually learned something. I told them that on the basis of their performance so far they should sue their previous teachers for malpractice. I told them that anyone who says "I know it, but I can't explain it" would flunk the course.

After an hour and a half they escaped, except for one of them, who came to my office for further instruction. Although it was the end of the third week, she was still not quite sure about the structure of the basic English sentence. (This, of course, was a reflection on me, not her.) I took her through the subject and predicate slots and she seemed to understand who or what an actor is and the relationship of the actor to the action performed, but she couldn't quite get the concept of the object of the action.

We were working with a sentence she had composed, "I threw the book into the garbage." I asked her, "In that sentence what is the relationship between 'threw' and 'book'?" She didn't know. I tried again: "What is the impact on the object of the action?" She didn't understand the question.

I decided that an illustration might do the trick; so I picked up a book on my desk and threw it. It hit a shelf of books a few feet away. She said nothing for a few seconds and then asked in a voice calmer than mine would have been, "Can I drop this course?" "Yes," I answered (hoping to escape prosecution), and she left—the one person in the entire week who managed to get away.

—⁓—

What is this all about? I wondered. What's driving me to do these things? I got part of the answer by looking up obsessive-compulsive disorder on the Internet and running down the list of symptoms. (Checking to see whether you have OCD is a form of OCD.) I found the following matches: fear of dirt; a need to have things just so; preoccupation with rules and schedules; rigidity; inflexibility; concern with order and symmetry; and saving containers when they are no longer needed. A perfect score.

And then it occurred to me that those are the very characteristics that make a dean effective: an obsessive need "to have things just so," a need to have things that are not right, put right.

What could I do aside from harassing perfectly innocent people who would have had every right to have me committed? Write this book was the answer. Although I was no longer in charge of a liberal arts college, I could satisfy my need to put the world in order by telling anyone who would listen how it should be done.

The first job, I decided, was to define the task. No serious reflection about an activity can get off the ground until the activity is characterized in a way that distinguishes it from all other activities. It is only when you know what the job is that you can know if you are really doing it, rather than doing some other job you were neither trained nor paid for.

It is when academics either don't know or have forgotten exactly what it is they are supposed to do that trouble begins, and criticisms of the academic enterprise multiply. These days, everyone, whether speaking from the left or the right, says the same thing—colleges and universities are in a sorry state, and ideology is the problem. One group finds ideology in the efforts of activists like David Horowitz, who wishes to monitor and alter the political make-up of the faculty, especially in the humanities and social sciences; while the other group finds ideology in the inability or unwillingness (these are two different arguments) of liberal faculty members to refrain from imposing their political views on students.

There's a lot of huffing and puffing on either side, and while I'm not writing to say, "a plague on both your houses," I am writing with the intention of carefully parsing the terms central to the controversy. Not because I hope to solve problems, but because I hope to dis-solve them, to suggest that the problems pretty much go away when you understand and act on a simple imperative—do your job—which comes along with two corollary imperatives—don't do somebody else's job and don't let someone else do your job.

So let us begin with a simple question. What exactly is the job of higher education and what is it that those who teach in colleges and universities are trained and paid to do? The two parts of the question have an obvious logical relationship: before you can speak sensibly about the scope and limits of a task, you have to know exactly what it is, what distinguishes it from other tasks. I put it that way because it is part of my argument that the coherence of tasks depends on their being distinctive. Think of it in consumer terms; you need something to be done, and you look in a phone book or search the Internet until you come upon a description of services that matches your need. What you want is a specialist, someone with the right training and credentials, and you might be suspicious if someone told you that he or she could do just about anything. To be sure, there are jacks of all trades, people who claim that they can do just about anything, and while that claim may prove out occasionally, more often than not you will feel most comfortable when you find a person or a company with a skill set that is reassuringly narrow: "this is what we do; we don't do those other things; but if this particular thing is what you want done, we're the people to turn to."

This narrow sense of vocation is shunned by many teaching in the academy today, and it was not popular in the 1960s when I was a young faculty member at the University of California at Berkeley. In the wake of the Free Speech Movement a faculty union had been formed and I had declined to join it. Some members of the steering committee asked me why, and I asked them to tell me about the union's agenda. They answered that the union would

(1) work to change America's foreign policy by fighting militarism, (2) demand that automobiles be banned from the campus and that parking structures be torn down, and (3) speak out strongly in favor of student rights. In response I said (1) that if I were interested in influencing government policy I would vote for certain candidates and contribute to their campaigns, (2) that I loved automobiles and wanted even more places to park mine, and (3) that I didn't see the point of paying dues to an organization dedicated to the interests of a group of which I was not a member. How about improvements in faculty salaries, better funding for the library, and a reduction in teaching load?

You, sir, I was admonished, do not belong in a university.

No, they didn't know what a university is and a lot of people still don't.

# ONE

# The Task of Higher Education

Pick up the mission statement of almost any college or university, and you will find claims and ambitions that will lead you to think that it is the job of an institution of higher learning to cure every ill the world has ever known: not only illiteracy and cultural ignorance, which are at least in the ball-park, but poverty, war, racism, gender bias, bad character, discrimination, intolerance, environmental pollution, rampant capitalism, American imperialism, and the hegemony of Wal-Mart; and of course the list could be much longer.

Wesleyan University starts well by pledging to "cultivate a campus environment where students think critically, participate in constructive dialogue and engage in meaningful contemplation" (although I'm not sure what meaningful contemplation is); but then we read of the intention to "foster awareness, respect, and appreciation for a diversity of experiences, interests, beliefs and identities." Awareness is okay; it's important to know what's out there. But why should students be taught to "respect" a diversity of interests, beliefs, and identities in advance of assessing them and taking their measure? The missing word here is "evaluate." That's what intellectual work is all about, the evaluation, not the celebration, of interests, beliefs, and identities; after all, interests can be base, beliefs can be wrong, and identities are often irrelevant to an inquiry.

Yale College's statement also starts well by promising to seek students "of all backgrounds" and "to educate them through mental discipline," but then mental discipline turns out to be instrumental to something even more valuable, the development of students'"moral, civic and creative capacities to the fullest." I'm all for moral, civic, and creative capacities, but I'm not sure that there is much I or anyone else could do as a teacher to develop them. Moral capacities (or their absence) have no relationship whatsoever to the reading of novels, or the running of statistical programs, or the execution of laboratory procedures, all of which can produce certain skills, but not moral states. Civic capacities—which mean, I suppose, the capacities that go along with responsible citizenship—won't be acquired simply because you have learned about the basic structures of American government or read the Federalist Papers (both good things to do). You could ace all your political science and public policy courses and still drop out and go live in the woods or become the Unabomber. And as for creative capacities, there are courses in creative writing in liberal arts colleges, and colleges of fine arts offer instruction in painting, sculpture, pottery, photography, drafting, and the playing of a variety of musical instruments. But even when such courses are housed in liberal arts venues, they belong more to the world of professional instruction—if you want to make something, here's how to do it—than to the world of academic interrogation. The discipline of Art History belongs to that world;

creating art does not. (I know this sounds circular—courses in creativity don't fit my definition of academic, so I deny them the label, but bear with me.)

Michigan State's statement promises everything. The university, it announces, will produce "an effective and productive citizen" who "contributes to society intellectually, through analytical abilities and in the insightful use of knowledge; socially, through an understanding and appreciation of the world and for individual group beliefs and traditions; ethically, through sensitivity and faithfulness to examined values; and politically through the use of reason in affairs of state." Aside from its ungrammaticalness ("understanding...for" is not an English construction), this ambitious mouthful confuses a hoped-for effect—graduates who perform admirably as citizens—with what can actually be taught. Analytical abilities can be taught as can knowledge, but "insightful use" is a matter of character, and character cannot be taught, at least not by Ph.D.'s in English or Chemistry. I don't know what "an appreciation of the world" means, and "individual group beliefs and traditions" is a pathetic and incoherent attempt to sit on the fence of at least three issues. As for examining values, that *is* a proper task for the academy, but ensuring "faithfulness" to values is not. How could such fidelity be measured, and who would be qualified to measure it? And one hopes of course that those charged with the management of our political destiny employ "reason" when conducting affairs of state, but whether they do won't depend on their having taken courses in symbolic logic.

So what is it that institutions of higher learning are supposed to do? My answer is simple. College and university teachers can (legitimately) do two things: (1) introduce students to bodies of knowledge and traditions of inquiry that had not previously been part of their experience; and

(2) equip those same students with the analytical skills—of argument, statistical modeling, laboratory procedure—that will enable them to move confidently within those traditions and to engage in independent research after a course is over.

If you think about it, that's a lot to ask. It's at least a full-time job and it wouldn't seem to leave much room for taking on a bunch of other jobs.

I'm not saying that there is no connection at all between the successful practice of ethical, social, and political virtues and the courses of instruction listed in the college catalogue; it's always possible that something you come across or something a teacher says may strike a cord that sets you on a life path you might not otherwise have chosen. But these are contingent effects, and as contingent effects they cannot be designed and shouldn't be aimed at. (It's not a good use of your time to aim at results you have only a random chance of producing.)

What can be designed are courses that introduce students to a demarcated field, reading lists that reflect the current state of disciplinary knowledge, exams or experiments that test the ability of students to extend what they have studied to novel fact situations, and in-class exercises that provoke students to construct and solve problems on their own. The designing of these (and related) structures and devices makes sense in the context of an aim that is specific to the pedagogical task—the aim of passing on knowledge and conferring skills.

Anyone who asks for more has enlisted in the "we-are-going-to-save-the world" army along with Derek Bok, the former president of Harvard and the author of *Our Underachieving Colleges*. Here is a partial list of the things Bok believes colleges and universities should be trying to achieve: "help develop such virtues as racial tolerance, honesty and social responsibility"; "prepare...students to be active, knowledgeable citizens in a democracy"; "nurture...good moral character." He notes that "college catalogues regularly announce an intention to go beyond intellectual pursuits to nurture such behavioral traits," but laments that some professors (I am one he cites) believe that the only proper ends of the university are those that involve "'the mastery of intellectual and scholarly skills.'"

My response is that the limited, focused nature of this latter aim—it has one target, not many or all—is what makes it at least potentially achievable. Teachers can, by virtue of their training and expertise, present complex materials in ways that make them accessible to novices. Teachers can also put students in possession of the analytical tools employed by up-to-date researchers in the field. But teachers cannot, except for a serendipity that by definition cannot be counted on, fashion moral character, or inculcate respect for others, or produce citizens of a certain temper. Or, rather, they cannot do these things unless they abandon the responsibilities that belong to them by contract in order to take up responsibilities that belong properly to others. But if they do that, they will be practicing without a license and in all likelihood doing a bad job at a job they shouldn't be doing at all. When that happens—and unfortunately it does happen—everyone loses. The students lose because they're not getting what they paid for (it will be said that they are getting more, but in fact they are getting less). The university loses because its resources have been appropriated for a nonacademic purpose. Higher education loses, because it is precisely when teachers offer themselves as moralists, therapists, political counselors, and agents of global change rather than as pedagogues that those who are on the lookout for ways to discredit higher education (often as a preliminary to taking it over) see their chance.

Does this mean that questions of value and discussion of current issues must be banished from the classroom? Not at all. No question, issue, or topic is off limits to classroom discussion so long as it is the object of academic rather than political or ideological attention. To many this will seem a difficult, if not impossible, distinction, but in fact, as I will argue in the following chapters, it is an easy one.

I should acknowledge up front that mine is a minority view and that any number of objections to it have appeared in the literature. There is the objection that what I urge is out of step both with history and with the best of current thinking. My argument, says Mark D. Gearen, president of Hobart and William Smith Colleges, "belies a rich history and deep tradition of civic responsibility within American Higher Education," a tradition, he adds, that is "articulated nearly universally in the mission statements of colleges and universities across the country" (Letter to the *New York Times*, May 24, 2004). In support of his position, President Gearen cites the 900 college and university executive officers who say, collectively, that "higher education has an unprecedented opportunity to influence the democratic knowledge, dispositions, and habits of the heart that graduates carry with them into the public sphere" ("Presidents' Declaration on the Civic Responsibility of Higher Education"). Nine hundred to one seems pretty conclusive, even if you add to my side worthies like Aristotle, Kant, Cardinal Newman, Max Weber, Learned Hand, Harry Kalven, John Hope Franklin, and Jacques Derrida. But we're not taking votes here; the merits or defects of my thesis should themselves be established by academic means, that is, by argument, and it is my argument—presented in the chapters of this book—that I am right and the nine hundred are wrong.

Chapter 2, "Do Your Job," lays out the general thesis: the academy's dignity and integrity depend on its being able to identify the task it properly performs. Thus my three-part mantra: do your job, don't try to do someone else's job, and don't let anyone else do your job.

Chapter 3, "Administrative Interlude," discusses the job of administrators separately because the work of administrators is often underappreciated and scorned. It is crucial that administrators understand what their role is in higher education, and I would argue, it is equally important that faculty understand what administrators make possible for them.

Chapter 4, "Don't Try to Do Someone Else's Job," insists that academics resist the temptation to take on extra-academic tasks, no matter how noble they may be. I'll clarify the doctrines of academic freedom and free speech, which are often understood (wrongly) to require (or allow) professors to step across the line I wish to draw between academic activity and partisan political activity. My deflationary definition of academic freedom is narrowly professional rather than philosophical, and its narrowness, I contend, enables it to provide clear answers to questions (about Holocaust Denial, Intelligent Design, polemical classroom rants) blurred by more ambitious definitions.

Chapter 5, "Don't Let Anyone Else Do Your Job," responds to the neoconservative attack on the academy and especially to the charge that left-leaning teachers are corrupting our youth by preaching relativism, atheism, and a disdain for truth. Neoconservatives want an academy where their politics are given a proportional representation (they call it balance or intellectual diversity) in the selection of texts and faculty members. I want an academy inflected by no one's politics, but by the nitty-gritty obligations of teaching and research.

Chapter 6 talks about the dangerous attempts by the government to withdraw funds from public education and exert more control over what it is no longer paying for. Chapter 7 revisits the basic issues.

The topics considered and arguments waged in these chapters vary, but everything follows from the wish to define academic work precisely and narrowly in opposition to those who would expand it to include everything under the sun and a few things above it. I take my text from a provost at the University of Wisconsin, Madison, who, in response to students demanding that the university declare a position on the then impending invasion of Iraq, said, "The University of Wisconsin does not have a foreign policy." Nor, I would add, does it have a domestic policy, or an environmental policy, or an economic policy, or any policy except an educational policy. The dangers inherent in a more expansive notion of what colleges and universities should be doing were dramatically illustrated in April 2006 when a major association of British higher education professors voted to boycott Israeli universities and refuse to do business with Israeli academics until they publicly disavowed the policies and practices of their government. The surrender of the academic enterprise to political considerations could not be more blatant. It might be thought that the practices I inveigh against in the following pages—announcing one's political allegiances in class, poking fun at the administration in power, railing against capitalism, giving the writing course over to discussions of various forms of discrimination—are, at least in comparison, less toxic and therefore less culpable. But as far as I am concerned they are the fruit of the same poisoned tree.

# TWO

# *Do Your Job*

So back to the basic question. What exactly is the job of someone who teaches in a college or a university? My answer is simple and follows from legal theorist Ernest Weinrib's account of what is required if an activity is to have its own proper shape. It must present itself "as a *this* and not a *that*."

## A THIS...

As I have already said, the job of someone who teaches in a college or a university is to (1) introduce students to bodies of knowledge and traditions of inquiry they didn't know much about before; and (2) equip those same students with the analytical skills that will enable them to move confidently within those traditions and to engage in independent research should they choose to do so.

Job performance should be assessed on the basis of academic virtue, not virtue in general. Teachers should show up for their classes, prepare lesson plans, teach what has been advertised, be current in the literature of the field, promptly correct assignments and papers, hold regular office hours, and give academic (not political or moral) advice. Researchers should not falsify their credentials, or make things up, or fudge the evidence, or ignore data that tells against their preferred conclusions. Those who publish should acknowledge predecessors and contributors, provide citations to their sources, and strive always to give an accurate account of the materials they present.

That's it, there's nothing else, and nothing more. But this is no small list of professional obligations, and faculty members who are faithful to its imperatives will have little time to look around for causes and agendas to champion.

## ...AND NOT A THAT

A faculty committee report submitted long ago to the president of the University of Chicago declares that the university exists "only for the limited...purposes of teaching and research" and reasons that "since the university is a community only for those limited and distinctive purposes, it is a community which cannot take collective action on the issues of the day without endangering the conditions for its existence and effectiveness" (Kalven Committee Report on the University's Role in Political and Social Action, November 11, 1967). Of course it can and should take collective (and individual) action on those issues relevant to the educational mission—the integrity of scholarship, the evil of plagiarism, and the value of a liberal education. Indeed failure to pronounce early and often on these matters would constitute a dereliction of duty. But neither the university as a collective nor its faculty as individuals should advocate personal, political, moral, or any other kind of views except academic views.

My point is not that academics should refrain from being political in an absolute sense—that is impossible—but that they should engage in the politics appropriate to the enterprise they signed onto. That means arguing about (and voting on) things like curriculum, department leadership, the direction of research, the content and manner of teaching—everything that is relevant to the responsibilities we take on when we accept a paycheck.

The distinction I am insisting on—between what a university properly stands for and what is, at most, tangential to its core activities—can be illustrated by the debate about free speech zones on campuses. Some activists on both the left and the right protest such zones and argue that the entire university should be a free speech zone, one large Hyde Park corner, for after all isn't the university primarily a place for the unfettered expression of ideas? The answer is no. The university is primarily a place for teaching and research. The unfettered expression of ideas is a cornerstone of liberal democracy; it is a prime political value. It is not, however, an academic value, and if we come to regard it as our primary responsibility, we will default on the responsibilities assigned us and come to be what no one pays us to be—political agents engaged in political advocacy.

The only advocacy that should go on in the classroom is the advocacy of what James Murphy has identified as the intellectual virtues, "thoroughness, perseverance, intellectual honesty," all components of the cardinal academic virtue of being "conscientious in the pursuit of truth" ("Good Students and Good Citizens," *New York Times*, September 15, 2002). A recent Harris Poll revealed that in the public's eye teachers are the professionals most likely to tell the truth; and this means, I think, that telling the truth is what the public expects us to be doing. If you're not in the pursuit-of-truth business, you should not be in the university.

I have been accused (by educational philosophers Elizabeth Kiss and Peter Euben) of ignoring "the vast and varied terrain of general undergraduate education, professional and vocational education, residential life, and extracurricular activity on America's college and university campuses." Yes, I ignore these activities, and the reason I do is captured in the word "extracurricular," that is, to the side of the curriculum. The core of a college or university experience should be the academic study of the questions posed by the various disciplines, but that core is surrounded by offices of housing, transportation, recreation, financial aid, advising, counseling, student services, and much more. Even though these activities support and in some instances make possible what goes on in the classroom and the laboratory, they are not academic. Therefore those who engage in them, either on the student side or the staff side, should not receive academic credit for doing so. I have no objection to internship programs, community outreach, peer tutoring, service learning, etc., as long as they are not thought of as satisfying graduation or grade requirements.

The exceptions one might think of do not weaken my point, but make it clearer: a student who returns from an internship experience and writes an academic paper (as opposed to a day-by-day journal or a "what-I-did-on-my-summer-vacation" essay) analyzing and generalizing on her experience, should get credit for it; and a student in a school of education who teaches in an inner city school under faculty supervision should certainly get credit for that; it is part of her academic training.

But what about professional schools and professional training? Kiss and Euben observe correctly that the "core mission" of professional education, as it is usually understood, inescapably involves influencing "students' behavior beyond [the] classroom" by putting them in possession of skills they are expected to apply directly in a specific line of work. If this is, in fact, what transpires in a particular professional school—if students are taught methods and techniques in the absence of any inquiry into their sources, validity, and philosophical underpinnings—that professional school is not the location of any intellectual activity and is "academic" only in the sense that it is physically housed in a university.

The question "is it academic or is it job training?" is endlessly debated in the world of law schools, where there is an inverse relationship between hands-on training (of the kind apprentices used to receive before there were law schools) and prestige. The more highly ranked the law school, the less its students will be put in touch with the nitty-gritty of actual practice and the more versed they will be in the arcana of interpretive theory, moral philosophy, Coasean economics, and even literary criticism. It is commonplace for graduates of top-ten law schools to report that the law school experience left them unprepared to deal with the tasks and problems they encountered as working lawyers. In response, a law school faculty might reply—and by so replying reinforce the distinction I have been insisting on—"We are intellectuals, not mechanics; what we do is teach you how to think about the things we think about, and what we prepare you for is life as a law professor; that's our job. The rest you get elsewhere."

## DRAWING THE LINE: ACADEMICIZING

There are many objections to this severe account of what academics should and shouldn't do, but one is almost always raised—how do you draw the line? Even if your intentions are good, how do you refrain from inadvertently raising inappropriate issues in the classroom? I call this the objection of impossibility, which takes two forms. One form says that teachers come to the classroom as fully developed beings who have undergone certain courses of instruction, joined political parties, embraced or refused religious allegiances, pledged themselves to various causes, and been persuaded to the truth of any number of moral or ideological propositions. In short, teachers believe something, indeed many things, and wouldn't it be impossible for them to detach themselves from these formative beliefs and perform in a purely academic manner? Wouldn't the judgments they offered and the conclusions they reached be influenced, if not largely determined, by the commitments I say they should set aside?

This objection contrives to turn the unavailability of purity—which I certainly acknowledge—into the impossibility of making distinctions between contexts and the behaviors appropriate to them. Even if it is the case that whatever we do is shaped to some extent by what we've done in the past, that past is filtered through the conventional differences by which we typically organize our daily lives. We understand, for example, that proper behavior at the opera differs from proper behavior at a ball game, and we understand too that proper behavior at the family dinner table differs from proper behavior at a corporate lunch. It would be possible to trace our actions in all of these contexts back to decisions made and allegiances formed long ago, but those actions would still be distinguishable from one another by the usual measures that mark off one social context from another. The fact that we bring a signature style, fashioned over many years, to whatever we do does not mean that we are always doing the same thing. We are perfectly capable of acting in accordance with the norms that belong to our present sphere of activity, even if our "take" on those norms is inflected somewhat by norms we affirm elsewhere.

But is it so easy to compartmentalize one's beliefs and commitments? Yes it is. In fact, we do it all the time when we refrain, for example, from inserting our religious beliefs or our private obsessions into every situation or conversation no matter what its content. Those who cannot or will not so refrain are shunned by their neighbors and made the object of satires by authors like Swift and Dickens. Setting aside the convictions that impel us in our political lives in order to take up the task of teaching (itself anchored by convictions, but ones specific to its performance) is not at all impossible, and if we fail to do it, it is not because we could not help ourselves, but because we have made a deliberate choice to be unprofessional.

The second form of the impossibility objection asserts that there can be no distinction between politics and the academy because everything is political. It is the objection that in many courses, especially courses given at a law school or by political science departments, the materials being studied are fraught with political, social, ethical, moral, and religious implications. How can those materials be taught at all without crossing the line I have drawn? Should they be excluded or allowed in only if they have first been edited so that the substantive parts are cut out? Not at all. I am not urging a restriction on content—any ideology, agenda, even crusade is an appropriate object of study. Rather I am urging a restriction on *what is done with the content* when it is brought into the classroom. If an idea or a policy is presented as a candidate for allegiance—aided by the instructor, students are to decide where they stand on the matter—then the classroom has been appropriated for partisan purposes. But if an idea or a policy is subjected to a certain kind of interrogation—what is its history? how has it changed over time? who are its prominent proponents? what are the arguments for and against it? with what other policies is it usually packaged?—then its partisan thrust will have been blunted, for it will have become an object of analysis rather than an object of affection.

In the fall of 2004, my freshman students and I analyzed a speech of John Kerry's and found it confused, contradictory, inchoate, and weak. Six weeks later I went out and voted for John Kerry. What I was doing in class was subjecting Kerry's arguments to an academic interrogation. Do they hang together? Are they coherent? Do they respond to the issues? Are they likely to be persuasive? He flunked. But when I stepped into the ballot box, I was asking another set of questions: Does Kerry represent or speak for interests close to mine? Whom would he bring into his administration? What are likely to be his foreign policy initiatives? How does he stand on the environment? The answers I gave to the first set of *academic* questions had no relationship whatsoever to the answers I gave to the second set of *political* questions. Whether it is a person or a policy, it makes perfect sense to approve it in one venue and disapprove it in another, and vice versa. You could decide that despite the lack of skill with which a policy was defended (an academic conclusion), it was nevertheless the right policy for the country (a political decision). In the classroom, you can probe the policy's history; you can explore its philosophical lineage; you can examine its implications and likely consequences, but you can't urge it on your students. Everything depends on keeping these two judgments, and the activities that generate them, separate.

Again, this is not to say that academic work touches on none of the issues central to politics, ethics, civics, and economics; it is just that when those issues arise in an academic context, they should be discussed in academic terms; that is, they should be the objects of analysis, comparison, historical placement, etc.; the arguments put forward in relation to them should be dissected and assessed *as* arguments and not as preliminaries to action on the part of those doing the assessing. The action one takes (or should take) at the conclusion of an academic discussion is the action of rendering an *academic* verdict as in "that argument makes sense," "there's a hole in the reasoning here," "the author does (or does not) realize her intention," "in this debate, X has the better of Y," "the case is still not proven." These and similar judgments are judgments on craftsmanship and coherence— they respond to questions like "is it well made?" and "does it hang together?" The judgment of whether a policy is the right one for the country is not appropriate in the classroom, where you are (or should be) more interested in the structure and history of ideas than in recommending them (or dis-recommending them) to your students. To be sure, the ideas will be the same whether you are dissecting them or recommending them; but dissecting them is what you are supposed to do if you are paid to be an academic. Recommending them is what you do when you are a parent, or a political activist, or an op-ed columnist, all things you may be when the school day ends, but not things you should be on the university's or state's dime.

It might be objected that while it may be easy to remain within academic bounds when the debate is about the right interpretation of *Paradise Lost*, the line between the academic and the political has been blurred before the discussion begins when the subject is ethics and students are arguing, for example, about whether stem cell research is a good or bad idea.

But students shouldn't be arguing about whether stem cell research is a good or bad idea. They should be studying the arguments various parties have made about stem cell research. Even in a class focused on ethical questions, the distinction I would enforce holds. Analyzing ethical issues is one thing; deciding them is another, and only the first is an appropriate academic activity. Again, I do not mean to exclude political topics from the classroom, but to insist that when political topics are introduced, they not be taught politically, that is, with a view to either affirming or rejecting a particular political position.

The name I give to this process whereby politically explosive issues are made into subjects of intellectual inquiry is "academicizing." *To academicize a topic is to detach it from the context of its real world urgency, where there is a vote to be taken or an agenda to be embraced, and insert it into a context of academic urgency, where there is an account to be offered or an analysis to be performed.*

Take, for example, a question that was much debated in newspapers and on talk shows during the second term of George W. Bush's presidency: is George W. Bush the worst president in our history? How could you academicize *that* question? Simple. Turn the question itself into an object of study. You might begin by inquiring into the American fascination, even obsession, with ranking. We rank everything: restaurants, movies, athletes, cities, national parks, automobiles, hotels, vacation spots, spas, beers, tennis racquets, golf clubs, novels, appliances, computers, cameras, malls, and of course colleges and universities. What's that all about? Is it because Americans are upwardly mobile and require tangible evidence of the heights to which they have or have not risen? Is it because in the absence of a fixed class structure we need some way to measure where we belong? After you've discussed the significance of ranking in American life, you can return to the ranking of presidents and pose some historical questions: When were the first rankings and what was the announced reason for making them? What kind of shift has there been in the rankings over the years? Whose stock has gone up and whose down and why? Do presidents themselves ever comment on their position in the ranking? What kinds of things do they say? The more this line of inquiry is pursued, the less the question "Is George W. Bush in fact the worst president in our history?" will be foregrounded. The urgency of that question—which is political—will have been replaced by the urgency to understand a phenomenon. The question will have been academicized.

Consider as another example the Terry Schiavo tragedy. How can this event in our national history be taught without taking sides on the issues it raises? Again, simple: discuss it as a contemporary instance of a tension that has structured American political thought from the founders to John Rawls—the tension between substantive justice, justice rooted in a strong sense of absolute right and wrong, and procedural justice, justice tied to formal rules that stipulate the steps to be taken and the persons authorized to take them. On one side were those who asked the question: what is the morally right thing to do about Terry Schiavo? On the other side there were those who asked the question: who is legally entitled to make the relevant decisions independently of whether or not we think those decisions morally justified? Once these two positions are identified, their sources can be located in the work of Locke, Kant, Mill, Isaiah Berlin, and others, and the relationship between those sources and the Schiavo incident can become the focus of analysis. As this is happening—as the subject is being academicized—there will be less and less pressure in the class to come down on one side or the other and more and more pressure to describe accurately and fully the historical and philosophical antecedents of both sides. A political imperative will have been replaced by an academic one. There is no topic, however politically charged, that will resist academicization. Not only is it possible to depoliticize issues that have obvious political content; it is easy.

But is it a good idea? The objection of impossibility often arrives in tandem with the objection of unworthiness. It says that even if it is possible to set aside one's political convictions when conducting a class, it would be unworthy to do so because it would be a dereliction of one's duty as a human being concerned with the well-being of the world. After all, the complaint goes, the times cry out for sane, informed voices and here are you urging the most educated and cosmopolitan segment of our population to remain silent.

Actually I am urging professors to remain silent on important political issues only when they are engaged in teaching. After hours, on their own time, when they write letters to the editor or speak at campus rallies, they can be as vocal as they like about anything and everything. That distinction is not likely to satisfy a critic like Ben Wallace, who complained on huffingtonpost.com (in response to a *New York Times* op-ed) that "under Fish's rule, a faculty member in the South in the 1950's could not embrace and urge the idea that segregation is wrong and that students should act to remedy the situation." That's right. In the 1950s the legal and moral status of segregation was a live political question working its way through legislatures and courts, which were (and are) the proper venues for adjudicating the issue. Faculty members were free to air their views in public forums and many did, but those who used the classroom as a soapbox were co-opting a space intended for other purposes. Today the situation is quite different. Segregation, at least the nonvoluntary kind, is no longer a live issue; it has been settled and there is no possibility at all of reviving it. Consequently it would now be entirely appropriate to discuss it in a classroom and even appropriate for a professor to declare (as some have declared of slavery) that it really wasn't so bad. The professor who said that would no doubt be challenged, but the challenge would be to an assessment of an historical event, not to a policy recommendation in the present. In the case of segregation there is no need to insist that the topic be academicized; history has already academicized it, which means that, in the truest sense of the word, it is now academic.

How do you know whether or not you are really academicizing? Just apply a simple test: am I asking my students to produce or assess an account of a vexed political issue, or am I asking my students to pronounce on the issue? Some cases are easy. The writing instructor who appended to his syllabus on Palestinian poetics the admonition "Conservative students should seek instruction elsewhere" was obviously defaulting on his academic responsibilities. So are those professors who skip a class in order to participate in a political rally; even if their students are not encouraged to attend the rally, a message is being sent, and it is the wrong message.

Some teachers announce their political allegiances up front and believe by doing so they inoculate their students against the danger of indoctrination. But the political affiliations of a teacher will be irrelevant if political questions are analyzed rather than decided in the classroom. Coming clean about your own partisan preferences might seem a way of avoiding politics, but it sends the message that in this class political judgments will be part of what's going on, and again that is the wrong message.

(It might seem that I have violated my own strictures when I acknowledged a few pages ago that I voted for John Kerry at the end of 2004. Am I not announcing my political allegiances? No, because I offered the anecdote as an example, not as a piece of political persuasion. I was reporting on a political act, but I was not performing one.)

The wrong message can be sent by institutions as well as by those they employ. The basic test of any action contemplated by a university should take the form of a simple question:

has the decision to do this (or not do this) been reached on educational grounds? Let's suppose the issue is whether or not a university should fund a program of intercollegiate athletics. Some will say "yes" and argue that athletics contributes to the academic mission; others will say "no" and argue that it doesn't. If the question is decided in the affirmative, all other questions—should we have football? should we sell sweatshirts? should we have a marching band?—are business questions and should be decided in business terms, not in terms of global equity. Once the university has committed itself to an athletic program it has also committed itself to making it as profitable as possible, if only because the profits, if there are any, will be turned into scholarships for student athletes and others.

The same reasoning applies to investment strategies. It is the obligation of the investment managers to secure the best possible return; it is not their obligation to secure political or social or economic justice. They may wish to do those things as private citizens or as members of an investment club, but as university officers their duty is to grow the endowment by any legal means available. The argument holds also for those in charge of maintenance and facilities. The goal should be to employ the best workers at the lowest possible wages. The goal should not be to redress economic disparities by unilaterally paying more than the market demands.

When a university sets wages, it sets wages, period (sometimes a cigar is just a cigar). The action has its own internal-to-the-enterprise shape, and while one could always abstract away from the enterprise to some larger context in which the specificity of actions performed within it disappears and everything one does is "taking a stand," it is hard to see that anything is gained except a certain fuzziness of reference. The logic—the logic of the slogan "everything is political"—is too capacious, for it amounts to saying that whenever anyone does anything, he or she is coming down on one side or another of a political controversy and "taking a stand." But there is a difference between a self-consciously political act (such as the one my wife performs when she refuses to purchase goods manufactured by companies engaged in or benefitting from research on animals) and an act performed with no political intention at all, although it, inevitably, has a political effect (at least by some very generous definition of what goes into the political). Universities can pay wages with two intentions: (1) to secure workers, whether faculty or staff, who do the job that is required and do it well and (2) to improve the lot of the laboring class. The first intention has nothing to do with politics and everything to do with the size of the labor pool, the law of supply and demand, current practices in the industry, etc. The second intention has everything to do with politics— the university is saying, "here we declare our position on one of the great issues of the day"—and it is not an intention appropriate to an educational institution.

Nor is it appropriate for universities to divest their funds because they morally disapprove of countries or companies. The University of California at Berkeley periodically debates the wisdom or morality of accepting tobacco money. What's wrong with tobacco money? One simple answer was given by Stanton Glantz, a professor of cardiology at the University of California, San Francisco, when he declared, "The tobacco companies are crooks."

His judgment was apparently backed up by a ruling in a Washington, D.C., district court. Judge Gladys Kessler asserted that the defendants, a number of tobacco companies, had (among other things) deceived the American people about the dangers of smoking and "distorted the truth about low-tar and light cigarettes . . . in order to achieve their goal—to make money." But a district court ruling is hardly definitive, and the companies are working on an appeal that will challenge both the facts in the decision and the jurisdiction of the court. Even if Judge Kessler's ruling is affirmed, it will establish not that the tobacco companies are crooks, but that in the course of marketing a legal product they engaged in misleading advertising and other questionable business practices.

If universities must distance themselves from any entity that has been accused of being ethically challenged, there will be a very long list of people, companies, and industries they will have to renounce as business partners: brokerage firms, pharmaceutical firms, online-gambling companies, oil companies, automobile manufacturers, real-estate developers, cosmetic companies, fast-food restaurants, Hewlett-Packard, Microsoft, Wal-Mart, Target, Martha Stewart, Richard Grasso, and George Steinbrenner. And if you're going to spurn companies involved with Sudan, what about North Korea, Iran, Syria, China, Columbia, the Dominican Republic, Venezuela, Argentina, Russia, Israel, and (in the eyes of many left-leaning academics) the United States? These lists are hardly exhaustive and growing daily. Taking only from the pure will prove to be an expensive proposition (even Walt Disney won't survive the cut) and time consuming too, as the university becomes an extension of Human Rights Watch.

But it's the principle of the thing, isn't it? "There are some things one needs to do based on principle," declared California regent Norman Pattiz. To my mind that's just the trouble—universities acting indiscriminately on principle. I'm not saying that universities should be unprincipled, but that the principles they adhere to and enforce should be the principles appropriate to their mission and not principles that belong to other enterprises. And by mission, I don't mean the overblown, grandiose claim to cure all ills and make the world better found in university mission statements, but the educational and pedagogical mission, the mission of teaching and research.

But what about truth? Isn't it the case that universities "are supposed to be about truth and not about fraud," as Professor Glantz insisted? Same answer: there are many things to be true or false about, and not all of them fall within the university's sphere. It is up to courts to determine whether the tobacco companies have acted fraudulently and to levy penalties if it is found that they have. The truths the university is pledged to establish and protect are truths about matters under academic study: Is string theory a powerful analytic tool or a fiction? Is Satan the hero of *Paradise Lost*? Do the voting patterns of senior citizens vary regionally? And those truths are unrelated to and unaffected by the truths, whatever they may be, about the business practices of tobacco companies.

But if you take their money, aren't you endorsing their ethics and in effect becoming a partner in their crimes? No. If you take their money, you're taking their money. That's all. The crimes they may have committed will be dealt with elsewhere, and as long as the funds have not been impounded and are in fact legally the possession of those who offer them, the act of accepting them signifies nothing more than appreciation of the gift and the intention to put it to good academic use.

So are there no circumstances in which a university should decline funds offered to it, except the circumstance of money legally (not morally) dirty? Yes, there is one— when the funds come with strings attached, when the donor says these are the conclusions I want you to reach, or these are the faculty I want you to hire, or these are the subjects I want you to teach or stop teaching. Every university already has a rule against accepting donations so encumbered, and it is a matter of record that tobacco companies abide by this restriction and do not expect (although they may hope) that their contributions will produce results friendly to their cause.

In fact there is only one funding source that attempts to exert control over what the university does with the money it receives, and that is the state legislatures and (in the case of private universities) the boards of trustees that are notorious for threatening to withdraw financial support unless the university gives the right courses and promotes or fires the right professors. That, as I will argue later, is the real danger to university integrity—not corporations skirting the edge of illegality or cozying up to repressive regimes, but the very people who are supposedly looking out for the enterprise and are instead trying to bend it to their purposes.

Sometimes the danger to institutional integrity comes from academics themselves when they try to bend the university to a political purpose. This is what happened at Southern Methodist University when it became clear that the campus was the likely location of the George W. Bush Presidential Library. (It's now a done deal.) Immediately, alumni and some faculty began to say things like, "I find it patently offensive for the Board [of SMU] to consider such an affront to justice given the Bush record," and "Do we want SMU to benefit from a legacy of massive violence?" and "Why on earth would you want anything with that man's name stamped on it?" A group of Methodist ministers, including some bishops, set up a Web site that asked members of the church and other concerned citizens to sign a petition indicating their disapproval of the proposed library. Two theology professors associated with the university complained in the student newspaper of "the secrecy of the Bush administration and its virtual refusal to engage with those holding contrary opinions" (could there be a more blatant instance of the pot calling the kettle black?) and asked, rhetorically, "what does it mean ethically to say that regardless of an administration's record and its consequences, it makes no difference when considering a bid for the library?"

What it means is that the question of the ethics of the Bush administration—does it condone torture? does it invade the privacy of American citizens? does it sacrifice the environment to the interests of the oil and gas industry?—is independent of the question, is it a good thing for there to be a public repository of the records of a national administration for the purposes of research and education? Once that question is answered in the affirmative—and any other answer is almost inconceivable—the ethical performance (along with the political, military, and economic performance) of the administration becomes a matter of study rather than something you are either affirming or rejecting. Historians do not require that men and women whose lives and works they chronicle be admirable; the requirement is that they be significant, and that is a requirement every president, of whatever party or reputation, meets by definition.

Some members of the SMU Perkins School of Theology announced, self-righteously, "We count ourselves among those who would regret to see SMU enshrine attitudes and actions widely deemed as ethically egregious." But SMU would not be "enshrining" any attitudes or actions by housing the library; rather it would be helping to assure that a set of historical attitudes and actions will be subject to scholarly analysis. "Ethically egregious" may or may not be the judgment history delivers on the Bush presidency, but the fact that some members of the SMU community have made that judgment (as others have at times made it of the Clinton, Reagan, Carter, Ford, Nixon, Truman, Eisenhower, and Roosevelt presidencies) was not a reason for them to say no to the library unless they believed (wrongly) that it is the job of a university to impose a moral litmus test on the materials it lets into its archives or classrooms.

That is exactly what many of the protestors did believe, and they cited as evidence SMU's Code of Ethics, which celebrates the "Pursuit of truth, Integrity in work, Respect for persons, Responsible use of resources, and Accountability." After all, one protestor declared, "Institutions of education are all about values." Yes they are, but the values they are about are academic values, not values in general. A university is pledged to determining the truth about the texts its faculty studies. It is not pledged to confining itself to texts of whose truthfulness it is convinced. A university is pledged to respect the persons of its employees, which means that it evaluates everyone by the same set of nondiscriminatory standards. It does not mean that it restricts the object of its academic attention to people and groups that do not discriminate. A university is pledged to use its resources—money, equipment, labor—responsibly, but neither the responsibility nor irresponsibility of those entities it chooses to study is something it is pledged to consider. Those who think that by insisting on a moral yardstick, the university protects its integrity have it all wrong; the university forsakes its integrity when it takes upon itself the task of making judgments that belong properly to the electorate and to history. A university's obligation is to choose things worthy of study, not to study only things that it finds worthy.

## WHAT'S LEFT?

But wouldn't a university uninvolved in the great issues of the day be a place without passion, where classrooms were bereft of lively discussion and debate?

Definitely not. While the urgency of the political question will fade in the classroom I have imagined, it will have become a far livelier classroom as a result. In the class-rooms I have in mind, passions run high as students argue about whether the religion clause of the First Amend-ment, properly interpreted, forbids student-organized prayers at football games, or whether the Rawlsian notion of constructing a regime of rights from behind a "veil of ignorance" makes sense, or whether the anthropological study of a culture inevitability undermines its integrity. I have seen students discussing these and similar matters if not close to coming to blows then very close to jump-ing up and down and pumping their fists. These students are far from apathetic or detached, but what they are attached to (this again is the crucial difference) is the *truth* of the position to which they have been persuaded, and while that truth, strongly held, might lead at some later time to a decision to go out and work for a candidate or a policy, deciding *that* is not what is going on in the classroom.

By invoking the criterion of truth, I've already answered the objection that an academicized classroom—a class-room where political and moral agendas are analyzed, not embraced—would be value-free and relativistic. If anything is a value, truth is, and the implicit (and sometimes explicit) assumption in the classroom as I envision it is that truth, and the seeking of truth, must always be defended. To be sure, truth is not the only value and there are others that should be defended in the contexts to which they are central; but truth is a pre-eminent *academic* value, and adherence to it is exactly the opposite of moral relativism. You will never hear in any of my classes the some-people-say-X-but-others-say-Y-and-who's-to-judge dance. What I strive to deter-mine, together with my students, is which of the competing accounts of a matter (an academic not a political matter) is the right one and which are wrong. "Right" and "wrong" are not in the lexicon of moral relativism, and the students who deliver them as judgments do so with a commitment as great as any they might have to a burning social issue.

Students who are asked to compare the models of heroism on display in the *Iliad*, the *Aeneid*, and Wordsworth's *Prelude*, or to chart the changes in the legal understanding of what the founders meant when they enjoined Congress from establishing a religion, will engage in discussions that are at least as animated as any they might have in the dorm room about some pressing issue of the day. It is only if you forget that academic questions have histories, and that those histories have investments, and that those investments are often cross- and interdisciplinary that you could make the mistake of thinking that confining yourself to them and resisting the lure of supposedly "larger" questions would make for an experience without spirit and energy.

Not only is the genuinely academic classroom full of passion and commitment; it is more interesting than the alternative. The really dull classroom would be the one in which a bunch of nineteen- or twenty-year-olds debate assisted suicide, physician-prescribed marijuana, or the war in Iraq in response to the question "What do you think?" Sure, lots of students would say things, but what they would say would be completely predictable—a mini-version of what you hear on the Sunday talk shows—in short, a rehearsing of opinions. Meanwhile the genuine excitement of an academic discussion where you have a chance of learning something, as opposed to just blurting out uninformed opinions, will have been lost. What teacher and student are jointly after is knowledge, and the question should never be "What do you think?" (unless you're a social scientist conducting a survey designed to capture public opinion). The question should be "What is the truth?" and the answer must stand up against challenges involving (among other things) the quality and

quantity of evidence, the cogency of arguments, the sound-
ness of conclusions, and so forth. At the (temporary) end
of the process, both students and teachers will have learned
something they didn't know before (you always know what
your opinions are; that's why it's so easy to have them) and
they will have learned it by exercising their cognitive capacities in ways that leave them exhilarated and not merely self-
satisfied. Opinion-sharing sessions are like junk food: they
fill you up with starch and leave you feeling both sated and
hungry. A sustained inquiry into the truth of a matter is an
almost athletic experience; it may exhaust you, but it also
improves you.

## A RADICAL PROPOSITION: TEACH WRITING IN WRITING CLASSES

Improvement of a particular skill is supposedly the point of
composition classes, but in no area of the curriculum has the
lure of supposedly larger questions proven stronger. More
often than not anthologies of provocative readings take center stage and the actual teaching of writing is shunted to the
sidelines. Once ideas are allowed to be the chief currency in
a composition course, the very point of the course is forgotten. That is why I say to my students on the first day of
class, "We don't do content in this class. By that I mean we
are not interested in ideas—yours, mine, or anyone else's. We
don't have an anthology of readings. We don't discuss current
events. We don't exchange views on hot-button issues. We
don't tell each other what we think about anything—except
about how prepositions or participles or relative pronouns
function." The reason my students and I don't do any of these
things is that once you begin talking about ideas, the focus is
shifted from the linguistic forms that make the organization
of content possible to this or that piece of content, usually

some recycled set of pros and cons about abortion, affirmative action, welfare reform, the death penalty, free speech, and so forth. At that moment, the task of understanding and mastering language will have been replaced by the dubious pleasure of reproducing the well-worn and terminally dull arguments one hears or sees on every radio and TV talk show.

Students who take so-called courses in writing where such topics are the staples of discussion may believe, as their instructors surely do, that they are learning how to marshal arguments in ways that will improve their compositional skills. In fact, they will be learning nothing they couldn't have learned better by sitting around in a dorm room or a coffee shop. They will certainly not be learning anything about how language works; and without a knowledge of how language works they will be unable either to spot the formal breakdown of someone else's language or to prevent the formal breakdown of their own.

In my classes, the temptation of content is felt only fleetingly; for as soon as students bend to the task of understanding the structure of language—a task with a content deeper than any they have been asked to forgo—they become completely absorbed in it and spontaneously enact the discipline I have imposed.

What exactly is that discipline? On the first day of my freshman writing class I give the students this assignment: you will be divided into groups and by the end of the semester each group will be expected to have created its own language, complete with a syntax, a lexicon, a text, rules for translating the text and strategies for teaching your language to fellow students. The language you create cannot be English or a slightly coded version of English, but it must be capable of indicating the distinctions—between tense, number, manner, mood, agency, and the like—that English enables us to make.

You can imagine the reaction of students who think that "syntax" is something cigarette smokers pay, guess that "lexicon" is the name of a rebel tribe inhabiting a galaxy far away, and haven't the slightest idea of what words like "tense," "manner" and "mood" mean. They think I'm crazy. Yet fourteen weeks later—and this happens every time— each group has produced a language of incredible sophistication and precision.

How is this near miracle accomplished? The short answer is that in the course of the semester the students come to understand a single proposition: a sentence is a structure of logical relationships. In its bare form, this proposition is hardly edifying, which is why I immediately supplement it with a simple exercise. "Here," I say, "are five words randomly chosen; turn them into a sentence." (The first time I did this the words were coffee, should, book, garbage, and quickly.) In no time at all I am presented with twenty sentences, all perfectly coherent and all quite different. Then comes the hard part. "What is it," I ask, "that you did? What did it take to turn a random list of words into a sentence?" A lot of fumbling and stumbling and false starts follow, but finally someone says, "I put the words into a relationship with one another."

Once the notion of relationship is on the table, the next question almost asks itself: what exactly are the relationships? And working with the sentences they have created the students quickly realize two things: first, that the possible relationships form a limited set; and second, that it all comes down to an interaction of some kind between actors, the actions they perform, and the objects of those actions.

The next step (and this one takes weeks) is to explore the devices by which English indicates and distinguishes between the various components of these interactions. If in every sentence someone is doing something to someone or something else, how does English allow you to tell who is the doer and who (or what) is the doee; and how do you know whether there is one doer or many; and what tells you that the doer is doing what he or she does in this way and at this time rather than another?

Notice that these are not questions about how a particular sentence works, but questions about how any sentence works, and the answers will point to something very general and abstract. They will point, in fact, to the forms that, while they are themselves without content, are necessary to the conveying of any content whatsoever, at least in English.

Once the students tumble to this point, they are more than halfway to understanding the semester-long task: they can now construct a language whose forms do the same work English does, but do it differently.

In English, for example, most plurals are formed by adding an "s" to nouns. Is that the only way to indicate the difference between singular and plural? Obviously not. But the language you create, I tell them, must have some regular and abstract way of conveying that distinction; and so it is with all the other distinctions—between time, manner, spatial relationships, relationships of hierarchy and subordination, relationships of equivalence and difference—languages permit you to signal.

In the languages my students devise, the requisite distinctions are signaled by any number of formal devices—word order, word endings, prefixes, suffixes, numbers, brackets, fonts, colors, you name it. Exactly how they do it is not the point; the point is that they know what it is they are trying to do; the moment they know that, they have succeeded, even if much of the detailed work remains to be done.

I recall the representative of one group asking me, "Is it all right if we use the same root form for adjectives and adverbs, but distinguish between them by their order in the sentence?" I could barely disguise my elation. If the students could formulate a question like that one, they had already learned the lesson I was trying to teach them.

It is a lesson that bears repeating. Just listen to *National Public Radio* for fifteen minutes or read a section of the *New York Times* and you will be able to start your own collection of howlers, from the (now ubiquitous) confusion of "disinterested" and "uninterested" (which sometimes takes the form of a parallel confusion of "disinvite" and "uninvite," the latter not an English verb form); to the disastrous and often comical substitution of "enervate" for "energize"; to the attribution of reticence to persons who are merely reluctant; to participles with no subjects or too many; to errors of pomposity ("between you and I," dubbed by a former colleague the "Cornell nominative"); to pronouns without referents or as many referents as there are nouns in the previous five sentences; to singular subjects with plural verbs (and the reverse); to dependent clauses attached to nothing; to mismatched tenses attached to the same action; to logical redundancies like, "The reason is because . . . " (I'm afraid I've been guilty of that one myself); not to mention inelegant repetitions and errors of diction made by people who seem to be writing a language they first encountered yesterday.

It seems that the art of speaking and writing precisely and with attention to grammatical form is less and less practiced. And I cannot claim that by writing this book, I will revive it. But I can offer some precepts that might at least improve the teaching of writing in our colleges and universities. All composition courses should teach grammar and rhetoric and nothing else. No composition course should have a theme, especially not one the instructor is interested in. Ideas should be introduced not for their own sake, but for the sake of the syntactical and rhetorical points they help illustrate, and once they serve this purpose, they should be sent away. Content should be avoided like the plague it is, except for the deep and inexhaustible content that will reveal itself once the dynamics of language are regarded not as secondary, mechanical aids to thought, but as thought itself. If content takes over, what won't get done is the teaching of writing, something the world really needs and something an academic with the appropriate training can actually do. But he or she won't ever get around to doing it if the class is given over to multiculturalism or racial injustice or globalization or reproductive rights or third-world novels or any of the other "topics," which, as worthy of study as they might be, take up all the air space and energy in the room and leave the students full of banal opinions but without the ability to use prepositions or write a clean English sentence.

The irony is that if you limit yourself to matters of composition and ask the students to confront the workings of language at the smallest level, you will have instructed them in something far deeper than all the hot-button issues that are initially so exciting and quickly become so boring.

How exactly would that instruction occur? What are its methods? A full answer would require a book of its own, but I can offer a small example of the process in action. One day I was talking with a law student who, although he had turned thirty-one the day before, didn't yet have a firm grasp of what a sentence is. I gave him my standard mantra—a sentence is a structure of logical relationships—but that didn't help. What did help—and usually helps, I find—is a return to basics so basic that it is almost an insult.

I asked him to write a simple three-word English sentence. He replied immediately: "Jane baked cookies." Give me a few more with the same structure, I said. He readily complied, but one of his examples was, "Tim drinks excessively." The next forty minutes were spent getting him to see why this sentence was not like the others (a kind of *Sesame Street* exercise), but he couldn't do that until he was able to see and describe the structure of sentences like, "Jane baked cookies."

I pointed to "baked" and asked him what function the word played. He first tried to tell me what the word meant. No, I said, the word's meaning is not relevant to an understanding of its function (meaning is always the enemy of writing instruction); I want to know what the word does, what role it plays in the structure that makes the sentence a sentence and not just a list of words. He fumbled about for a while and finally said that "baked" named the action in the sentence. Right, I replied, now tell me what comes along with an action. Someone performing it, he answered. And in the sentence, who or what is performing the action? "Jane," he said happily. Great! Now tell me what function the word "cookies" plays. Progress immediately stalled.

For a long time he just couldn't get it. He said something like, " 'Cookies' tells what the sentence is about." No, I said, that's content and we're not interested in content here (content is always the enemy of writing instruction); what I want to know is what structural relationship links "cookies" to the other parts of the sentence. More confusion. I tried another tack. What information does "cookies" provide? What question, posed implicitly by another of the sentence's components, does it answer? It took a while, but that worked. It answers the question, "What was baked?" he offered. Yes, I said, you've almost got it. Now explain in abstract terms that would be descriptive of any sentence with this structure, no matter what its content or meaning, the structural logic that links a word like "baked," a word that names an action, to a word like "cookies." More fumbling, but then he said "cookies" is what is acted upon. It was only then that I told him that in the traditional terminology of grammar, the thing acted upon is called the object. Had I given him the term earlier, he would have nodded, but he wouldn't have understood a thing. Now, he had at least the beginning of an understanding of how sentences are constructed and what work a sentence does; it organizes relationships between actors, actions, and things acted upon.

We still had to deal with "Tim drinks excessively," but at least there was something to build on. Does "excessively" name what is acted upon by the action "drinks"? No, he replied. What, then, does it do? A relapse into content: it tells what's happening. That's what "drinks" does, I reminded him. What information, in relation to "drinks" as a word with a specific function, does "excessively" provide? It was coming more quickly now. It tells us in what way he drinks, he said. Yes, the function of "excessively," and of any other word occupying the same structural slot, is to tell you something about the manner in which an action is performed. Oh, he said, an adjective. No, an adverb, I replied, but the term is less important than your understanding of the structural role. Does that mean, he asked, that the adverbial role can be played by more than one word, by many words? Now we were rolling.

I drove home the point of the lesson so far by asking him two simple questions. How many sentences, with different contents, are there that display the structures actor-action-acted upon or actor-action-manner of action? An infinite number, he replied. How many forms of the two structures are there? Only one, he said. Now you know, I told him, that form comes first, content second. If you grasp the abstract structural form of sentences like these, you can produce millions of them; you can organize any content whatsoever by imposing on it the logic of these forms.

The next exercise was considerably more sophisticated, but he completed it more quickly. Write a sentence that begins with the phrase "even though." No problem at all. He produced a bunch of them, including, "Even though I stayed up all night, I wasn't tired." How many "even though" sentences exist out there? I asked. He knew the drill: an infinite number. And how many forms? One. Now came the hard part. Describe that form without reference to any particular content. Describe, that is, the structure of every "even though" sentence ever written.

He quickly saw that the answer lay in the relationship between the two clauses (which he called "phrases"), but he had a hard time saying what the relationship was. He came up with the idea of contradiction but agreed that contradiction was too strong. He thought about it some and settled on a word he was familiar with as a law student. The second clause, he said, is a rebuttal of the first. Almost there. What does it rebut? It rebuts, he replied, what you would expect to follow from the first clause. You mean, I said (offering more help than I should have, but the afternoon was disappearing), that the second clause undoes in some way the expectation produced by the first. He acknowledged that this is what he meant.

What if the sentence read, "Even though I stayed up all night, I was tired." Oh, he replied, that wouldn't be a good "even though" sentence because the second part would say exactly what you would have expected it to say. How about if the sentence were just, "I stayed up all night; I wasn't tired." What would the difference be? He got it immediately. You wouldn't know from the beginning that the expectation produced by the first part is going to be disappointed. Isn't a sentence that begins with "notwithstanding" somewhat like an "even though" sentence? he wondered. You bet! End of the second lesson, except for my pointing out to him that while he always knew how to generate "even though" sentences and was capable of identifying misuses of the form, he now was able to describe the form and understand precisely how it works.

My assumption in all of this was that this analytical alertness to form, this ability to recognize forms and know when they are properly or improperly deployed, would translate into a greater alertness to the operations of form in his own writing. That assumption has not yet been tested empirically, but it should be noted that none of the more substantive, content-based approaches to the task seem to teach writing at all. We've now had decades of composition courses in which students do little but exchange their ill-informed views, and student writing has only gotten worse. Doesn't it make sense to think that if you are trying to teach them how to use linguistic forms, linguistic forms are what you should be teaching?

This discussion of the teaching of writing might seem to be a digression from my main task of identifying appropriate and inappropriate forms of pedagogical behavior. But in fact, the present state of composition studies is the clearest example of the surrender of academic imperatives to the imperatives of politics. Those instructors who turn their courses over to discussions of oppression and the evils of neoliberalism say things like "teaching grammatical rules is a form of social indoctrination," and "notions of correctness are devices by means of which the powers that be extend their illegitimate hegemony." In classrooms where these are the mantras, the subordination of academic work to the work of ideology is complete before the first lesson has been taught.

## BLURRING THE LINE

If you're doing academic rather than political work, you are, as I've said repeatedly, producing accounts and descriptions, rather than urging courses of action or taking a stand on some great question of the day. But hewing to the line I have drawn between analysis and advocacy is no guarantee that those who read or hear you will recognize and appreciate what you are doing. Someone who finds the distinction either opaque or false may well receive your disinterested analyses as if they were recommendations. You may be just expounding and defending academic views, but you will be heard as doing something more sinister. This is what happened to me in 2002, when I was accused of promoting terrorists' views and even of being a kind of terrorist myself. The accusation was made by another academic, a man named John Carey. Carey is a professor at Oxford and in September of 2002 he published a piece in the London *Times Literary Supplement* entitled "A Work in Praise of Terrorism? September 11 and *Samson Agonistes*." Carey described me (or rather my views) as "monstrous" and wondered why, unlike most people with "common humanity," I failed to condemn "mass murder."

Why would anyone say such things about an English teacher? What was my crime? Well, it turns out that my crime was that I had published a reading of John Milton's poetic drama *Samson Agonistes*, a retelling of the story of the biblical Samson who pulled down the supporting pillars of a Philistine temple, thereby killing, along with himself, thousands of men, women, and children he had never met. What drew Carey's ire is that in my reading of the play I declare Samson's act to be praiseworthy because he performed it in the conviction, or at least the hope, that it was what God wanted him to do. No, Carey protested, that can't be what Milton intended us to understand, for if it were, he would not be a great poet, but a murderous bigot, and anyone who, like Stanley Fish, says otherwise must himself be an apologist for murderous bigots and an advocate of violence to boot.

Now Carey can only come to this conclusion because he thinks that by offering an interpretive account of Samson's act, I endorse its morality and endorse by analogy other acts of religiously inspired violence, including the acts perpetrated by those who brought down the World Trade Towers. Were this so, I would be a very bad boy indeed, but in fact I endorse nothing except the correctness of my reading. I don't say, "religiously inspired violence is good"; I say that religiously inspired violence is what's going on in *Samson Agonistes*, and I say too that Milton does not encourage us to condemn it. That's a debatable reading, but it is a reading and not the declaration of my personal moral position. The proper response to my reading on the part of someone who disagrees with it would be first to say that it is wrong, and then to give reasons and cite evidence in support of that judgment. It is not a proper response to call me names and accuse me of besmirching the reputation of a great poet, as if a poet could only be great if he displayed sentiments approved of by John Carey. Neither I nor Milton should be attacked on the basis of the policies we are recommending, for neither of us is recommending any policies. He's writing a poem. I'm interpreting one.

Carey's mistake is the one that is the target of my argument on every page of this book. He confuses an academic argument with the practice of politics and conflates the writing of a poem with the publishing of a manifesto. Thus he declares that if Fish is right and *Samson Agonistes* does in fact condone religiously inspired violence, the play should be "withdrawn from schools and colleges, and indeed banned more generally as an incitement to terrorism." Neither *Samson Agonistes* nor I condone anything, and the only thing the play incites is reading, and along with reading a reflective stance toward the issues it dramatizes. "Reflective" is the key word, because it names both what poets do—reflect on matters like the relationship between political action and religious commitment—and what interpreters do in return—trace out the shape of reflection as it poses problems and teases them out to their edges. The exploration of problems, not their solution, and certainly not a program of political action, is what poetry offers. And if we take up that offer, our reward is not a recipe for dealing with the next crisis in our lives but a deepened understanding of the questions and moral conundrums the poet presents for our contemplation. Poems don't ask you to do anything except read them and be responsive to the intricacies of their unfolding.

If Milton's poetry is to be withdrawn from the schools, it should not be because its message is dangerous—having a message is not the business it's in—but because it fails to perform the business of poetry, the business of providing oases of reflection amid the urgencies that press in on us when we are being citizens, parents, politicians, soldiers, entrepreneurs, lawyers, doctors, engineers, etc.

## WHAT'S THE USE?

I have gone on at such length about poetry and what is appropriate to it because poetry is the liberal arts activity par excellence. Indeed, when liberal arts education is doing its job properly, it is just like poetry because, like poetry, it makes no claims to efficacy beyond the confines of its performance. A good liberal arts course is not good because it tells you what to do when you next step into the ballot box or negotiate a contract. A good liberal arts course is good because it introduces you to questions you did not know how to ask and provides you with the skills necessary to answer them, at least provisionally. And what do you do with the answers you arrive at? What do you do with the habits of thought that have become yours after four or more years of discussing the mind/body problem, or the structure of DNA, or Firmat's theorem, or the causes of World War I? Beats me! As far as I can tell those habits of thought and the liberal arts education that provides them don't enable you to do anything, and, even worse, neither do they prevent you from doing anything.

The view I am offering of higher education is properly called deflationary; it takes the air out of some inflated balloons. It denies to teaching the moral and philosophical pretensions that lead practitioners to envision themselves as agents of change or as the designers of a "transformative experience," a phrase I intensely dislike. I acknowledge a sense in which education can be transformative. A good course may transform a student who knew little about the material in the beginning into a student who knows something about it at the end. That's about all the transformation you should or could count on. Although the debates about what goes on in our colleges and universities are often conducted as if large moral, philosophical, and even theological matters are at stake, what is really at stake, more often than not, is a matter of administrative judgment with respect to professional behavior and job performance. Teaching is a job, and what it requires is not a superior sensibility or a purity of heart and intention—excellent teachers can be absolutely terrible human beings, and exemplary human beings can be terrible teachers—but mastery of a craft. Teachers who prefer grandiose claims and ambitions to that craft are the ones who diminish it and render it unworthy.

A convenient summary of the grandiose claims often made for teaching can be found in an issue of the journal *Liberal Education*. Here are some sentences from that issue:

- A classroom that teaches the virtues of critical analysis and respectful debate can go at least some way to form citizens for a more deliberative democracy.
- A liberal arts college or university that helps young people to learn to speak in their own voices and to respect the voices of others will have done a great deal to produce thoughtful and potentially creative world citizens.
- The aims of a strong liberal education include...shaping ethical judgment and a capacity for insight and concern for others.
- Contemporary liberal education must look beyond the classroom to the challenges of the community, the complexities of the workplace, and the major issues in the world.
- Students need to be equipped for living in a world where moral decisions must be made.

To which I respond, no, no, no, no, and no. A classroom that teaches critical analysis (sometimes called "critical thinking," a phrase without content) will produce students who can do critical analysis; and those students, no matter how skillfully analytical they have become, will not by virtue of that skill be inclined to "respect the voices of others." Learning how to perform in the game of argument is no guarantee either of the quality or of the morality of the arguments you go on to make. Bad arguments, bad decisions, bad actions are as available to the members of Phi Beta Kappa as they are available to the members of street gangs. And moreover, as I said earlier, respecting the voices of others is not even a good idea. You shouldn't respect the voices of others simply because they *are* others (that's the mistake of doctrinaire multiculturalism); you should respect the voices of those others whose arguments and recommendations you find coherent and persuasive.

And as for ethical judgment in general, no doubt everything you encounter helps to shape it, but reading novels by Henry James is not a special key to achieving it; and indeed—and there are many examples of this in the world— readers of Henry James or Sylvia Plath or Toni Morrison can be as vile and as cruel and as treacherous as anyone else. And if students "need to be equipped for living in a world where moral decisions must be made," they'd better seek the equipment elsewhere, perhaps from their parents, or their churches, or their synagogues, or their mosques. Nor can I agree that "contemporary liberal education must look beyond the classroom to the challenges of the community"; for it is only one short step from this imperative to the assertion that what goes on in the liberal arts classroom is merely preliminary to what lies beyond it, one short step to the judgment that what goes on in the liberal arts classroom acquires its value from what happens elsewhere; and then it is no step at all to conclude that what goes on in the liberal arts classroom can only be *justified* by an extracurricular payoff.

And here we come to the heart of the matter, the justification of liberal education. You know the questions: Will it benefit the economy? Will it fashion an informed citizenry? Will it advance the cause of justice? Will it advance anything? Once again the answer is no, no, no, and no. At some level of course, everything we ultimately do has some relationship to the education we have received. But if liberal arts education is doing *its* job and not the job assigned to some other institution, it will not have as its aim the bringing about of particular effects in the world. Particular effects may follow, but if they do, it will be as the unintended consequences of an enterprise which, if it is to remain true to itself, must be entirely self-referential, must be stuck on itself, must have no answer whatsoever to the question, "what good is it?" In a wonderful essay titled "What Plato Would Allow" (*Nomos* XXXVII, 1995), political theorist Jeremy Waldron muses about the appropriate response to someone who asks of philosophers, "What's the point of your work?" or "What difference is it going to make?" He replies (and I agree completely with him) that "we are not really doing...philosophy, and thus paradoxically...we are probably not really being of much use, unless we are largely at a loss as to how to answer that question."

Daniel Cottom comes to the same conclusion in his book *Why Education Is Useless*. His argument is that the accusation of inutility should be affirmatively embraced. "We should have done with the attempt to declare that education is useful," if only because "declarations of its usefulness prove to be beneath contempt." Cottom and I, however, part company on a crucial point. Whereas I reject justifying academic work because to do so means to deny it its own value—the value that leads people to take it up in the first place—Cottom turns the difficulty of justification into a positive virtue and therefore into a back-door form of justification. What he does is romanticize the inutility of academic work and celebrate it as a necessary counterweight to everything that is wrong with modern life. "We ought to celebrate the uselessness at the core of higher education and we should do so by seeing in the institutionalization of this uselessness a standing cultural commitment against the tyranny of stupidity in any form: the market, technocracy, the state, even the people." There is more than a whiff of academic exceptionalism here, the seductive and self-enhancing idea that professors are rarified creatures who, by virtue of their immersion in the library and the laboratory, are immune to the temptations and vulgarities to which lesser mortals fall. But it is no part of my intention to glorify or politicize the inutility of academic work. I just want to say that inutility is a fact about it, and a defining, not a limiting, fact. An unconcern with any usefulness to the world is the key to its distinctiveness, and this unconcern is displayed not in a spirit of renunciation (priesthood is not the goal here), but in a spirit of independence and the marking of territory.

An activity whose value is internal to its performance will have unpredictable and unintended effects in the world outside the classroom. But precisely because they are unpredictable and unintended, it is a mistake to base one's teaching on the hope of achieving them. On more than one occasion I have had an experience many professors will recognize. A student you haven't seen in years rushes up to you and says, "Oh, Professor, I think so often of that class in 1985 (or was it 1885?) when you said X and I was led by what you said to see Y and began on that very day to travel the path that has now taken me to success in profession Z. I can't thank you enough!"

You, however, are appalled, because you can't imagine yourself ever saying X (in fact you remember spending the entire semester saying anti-X) and you would never want anyone to exit from your class having learned Y (a lesson you have been preaching against for twenty years) and you believe that everyone would be better off if profession Z disappeared from the face of the earth. What, you might ask, did I do wrong?

The correct answer is quite likely, "nothing." It is the question that is wrong because it assumes that we are responsible for the effects of our teaching, whereas, in fact, we are responsible only for its appropriate performance. That is, we are responsible for the selection of texts, the preparation of a syllabus, the sequence of assignments and exams, the framing and grading of a term paper, and so on.

If by the end of a semester you have given your students an overview of the subject (as defined by the course's title and description in the catalogue) and introduced them to the latest developments in the field and pointed them in the directions they might follow should they wish to inquire further, then you have done your job. What they subsequently do with what you have done is their business and not anything you should be either held to account for or praised for. (Charlton Heston once said to Lawrence Olivier, "I've finally learned to ignore the bad reviews." "Fine," Olivier replied, "now learn to ignore the good ones.")

The question of what you are responsible for is also the question of what you should aim for, and what you should aim for is what you *can* aim for—that is, what you can reasonably set out to do as opposed to what is simply not within your power to do.

You can reasonably set out to put your students in possession of a set of materials and equip them with a set of skills (interpretive, computational, laboratory, archival), and even perhaps (although this one is really iffy) instill in them the same love of the subject that inspires your pedagogical efforts. You won't always succeed in accomplishing these things— even with the best of intentions and lesson plans there will always be inattentive or distracted students, frequently absent students, unprepared students, and on-another-planet students—but at least you will have a fighting chance given the fact that you've got them locked in a room with you for a few hours every week for four months.

You have little chance (and that entirely a matter of serendipity), however, of determining what they will make of what you have offered them once the room is unlocked for the last time and they escape first into the space of someone else's obsession and then into the space of the wide, wide world.

And you have no chance at all (short of a discipleship that is itself suspect and dangerous) of determining what their behavior and values will be in those aspects of their lives that are not, in the strict sense of the word, academic. You might just make them into good researchers. You can't make them into good people, and you shouldn't try.

Of course, somewhere down the line the answer a student once gave to an academic question may factor into the moral response he or she gives in a real-life crisis; but down the line is a long distance away, and meanwhile both faculty members and students will do well to remember the point of the enterprise they are *now* a part of.

Earlier I said that the liberal arts are like poetry because they make no claim to benefits beyond the pleasure of engaging in them. They are also like virtue because they are their own reward. That is, the reward is here and now, not some intangible benefit—wisdom, grace, gravitas—you will reap later. If you are committed to an enterprise and have internalized its values, you don't spend much time asking questions like "what is this good for?" You have already answered that question by sticking with the job: it's good because it's what you like to do.

# THREE

# *Administrative Interlude*

But you can't do it in a vacuum. And although academics would be reluctant to admit it, the conditions that make what they do possible are established and maintained by administrators. When I was a dean, the question I was most often asked by faculty members was, "Why do administrators make so much more money than we do?" The answer I gave was simple: administrators work harder, they have more work to do, and they actually do it.

At the end of my tenure as dean, I spoke to some administrators who had been on the job for a short enough time to be able still to remember what it was like to be a faculty member and what thoughts they had then about the work they did now. One said that she had come to realize how narcissistic academics are: an academic, she mused, is focused entirely on the intellectual stock market and watches its rises and falls with an anxious and self-regarding eye. As an academic, you're trying to get ahead; as an administrator, you're trying "to make things happen for other people"; you're "not advancing your own profile, but advancing the institution, and you're more service oriented."

A second new administrator reported that he finds faculty members "unbelievably parochial, selfish, and self-indulgent." They believe that their time is their own even when someone else is paying for it. They say things like "I don't get paid for the summer." They believe that they deserve everything and that if they are ever denied anything, it could only be because an evil administrator has committed a great injustice. Although they are employees of the university (and in public universities, of the state), they consider themselves independent contractors engaged fitfully in free-lance piecework. They have no idea of how comfortable a life they lead.

Neither, said a third administrator recently up from the ranks, do they have any idea of how the university operates. They seem proud of their parochialism and boast of their inability to access the many systems that hold the enterprise together. Ignorance of these matters is not a failing, but a badge of honor. Their first response to budget crises is to call for a cut in the administration, although, were the administrators to disappear, they wouldn't be able to put one foot in front of the other.

Although it would shock faculty members to hear it said, administration is an intellectual task, for it requires the ability to solve problems across a range of contexts without ever losing sight of the larger vision in which those contexts live and move and have their being. Here's a typical scenario. In one year in my time in the dean's office, the campus took a hit of about 10 percent, many millions of dollars. At that moment the college's revenues (95 percent state dollars) totaled about fifty-three million, forty-eight of which was earmarked for salaries. That left five million for everything else: operating expenses, new programs, new hires, additional instruction, etc. Obviously, a 10 or 12 percent additional cut would have left us unable either to pay the salaries already on the books or to provide the instruction mandated by the same folks who would be mandating the cut. (Political officials keep making statements about "fat" and scraping the "bottom of the barrel"; but they are either ignorant or dishonest or both; there is no fat and the barrel was scraped clean some time ago.)

What makes the problems administrators face more complicated and intractable than the problems faculty members face is the difficulty of getting a handle on them. Since budget figures constitute a moving target, they cannot be used to determine what wiggle room, if any, a dean or a provost might have when thinking about searches that have been authorized but not yet concluded. Should they be cancelled by an administration that would then display fiscal prudence in a climate that will applaud it but probably not reward it, or should the searches be allowed to continue with the risk that the administrators will be thought irresponsible? Should an administrator use what little he or she has to strengthen departments already strong? Or should the administrator shore up weak departments on the reasoning that this may be their last chance for a while to get any help? Eventually, an administration will move to something like a resolution, and then spend the next three years watching the results that will indicate whether the right people were disappointed (no matter what you do, somebody—often nearly everybody— will be unhappy).

To be sure, not all situations administrators face are that momentous or dramatic, but almost all of them involve problems of coordination that require calculations of incredible delicacy made in relation to numerous (and sometimes potentially conflicting) institutional goals and obligations. To whom shall we assign space, that most precious of academic commodities? How shall we adjudicate between the need for more offices, more labs, more homes for interdisciplinary work, more student and faculty lounges? If space becomes available in a remote building, should we provide relief to a space-poor department by sending some of its members to that outpost, or would that relief be the cause of even greater ills (loss of community, divided government, etc.)? An alternative might be to relocate the entire department, but if we did that, would we risk losing the benefits (casual but productive conversations, access to each other's seminars and lectures, opportunities for team teaching) proximity brings?

Another set of issues administrators face lies at the intersection of the professional and the personal. A complaint is made by a faculty member against his or her chair. The matter is not so grave as to constitute a grievance within the university guidelines, but is serious enough to threaten the internal health of the department. Do you speak to each of the parties separately and set yourself up as a judge of conflicting evidence, or do you call them both in and practice therapy without a license? Should you be attentive to the human dimension of the situation and worry about who is feeling pain about what, or should you be responsive only to the needs of the institution and settle for a truce that leaves everyone's hostile emotions in place? ("You guys may continue to hate each other, but you must agree to act with professional courtesy, even if you do so with gritted teeth.") Should you regard the present situation as a closed system or should you inquire into the prior behavior of the combatants with a view to determining whether one of them is a "bad egg" always looking for trouble? Or should you decide that to do any of these things would be to do too much and simply inform the chair about the disgruntled colleague and say, in effect, you deal with it, it's your job. (Unfortunately, if you opt for this strategy and let the cup pass, it will end up on your desk anyway.)

My point, I trust, is obvious: in the course of making a decision, an administrator must perform a complex act of taking into account any number of goals (short and long range), constituencies, interests, opportunities, costs, dangers; and at every point in a somewhat abstract calculation he or she must keep constantly in mind the forces and resources that must be marshaled (if they in fact can be) if the course of action decided upon is to be implemented in a way that leaves intact one's ability to deal flexibly with the next situation, and the next, and the next. This is what I meant when I said earlier that administration is an intellectual task: it requires the capacity to sift through mounds of data while at the same time continually relating what the data reveal to the general principles and aspirations of the enterprise.

So when faculty members ask what are administrators needed for anyway, the answer should be obvious: to develop, put in place, and, yes, administer the policies and procedures that enable those who scorn them to do the work they consider so much more valuable than the work of administration. If it weren't for administrators, there would be no class schedules and therefore no classes to teach, no admissions office and therefore no students to dazzle, no facilities management and therefore no laboratories to work in, no tenure process and therefore no security of employment, no budget officers and therefore no funds for equipment, travel, lectures, and teaching awards.

## ADVICE

If the administrative task is so complex and varied in its demands, how is anyone ever to learn how to do it? Mostly it's on-the-job training, but there are a few precepts that might be helpful.

Whenever a shoddy practice is allowed to continue even for a day, when an office is unresponsive, or a faculty member irresponsible, or a maintenance crew slipshod, or an elevator broken, or a phone system inefficient, everyone's morale suffers even if no one is conscious of it, and it is your job as an administrator to pursue the problem and insist that it be fixed even when it is located in a sphere over which you have no authority. Not only should you fight every battle, you should look for battles to fight, for what Conrad called the "flabby devil" is always settling into some corner of your world and you must always be ready to root him out.

The conventional wisdom says, "Keep your eye on the big picture." Don't sweat the details, delegate, and don't try to take care of everything.

Wrong.

If the pressure to do things right does not emanate from your office, it will not emanate from anywhere. If a department is not answering its phone, go to the office and find out why. If a class is not being met regularly, call in the instructor. If a light bulb has not been replaced in a few days, bug building and grounds. If old furniture clutters the halls, have it removed. If a classroom's walls are peeling, arrange to have it painted. If lectures are ill attended, do everything you can to get the people out, including coercing them. If the bookstore is inadequate, agitate. If there are no places on campus to sit down, figure out ways to put in some seating on the cheap. Do everything you can every day.

This, of course, is a recipe for burnout, but burning out is what administrators are supposed to do. That is why the shelf-life of administrators is about as short as the careers of NFL running backs, and for the same reason: they take too many hits.

# FOUR

# Don't Try to Do
# Someone Else's Job

Some of the hits taken by administrators will be delivered by those faculty members who have forgotten (or never knew) what their job is and spend time trying to form their students' character or turn them into exemplary citizens.

I can't speak for every academic, but I am not trained to do these things, although I am aware of people who are: preachers, therapists, social workers, political activists, professional gurus, inspirational speakers. Teachers, as I have said repeatedly, teach materials and confer skills, and therefore don't or shouldn't do a lot of other things—like produce active citizens, inculcate the virtue of tolerance, redress injustices, and bring about political change. Of course a teacher might produce some of these effects—or their opposites—along the way, but they will be, or should be, contingent and not what is aimed at. The question that administrators often ask, "What practices provide students with the knowledge and commitments to be socially responsible citizens?" is not a bad question, but the answers to it should not be the content of a college or university course. No doubt, the practices of responsible citizenship and moral behavior should be encouraged in our young adults, but it's not the business of the university to do so, except when the morality in question is the morality that penalizes cheating, plagiarizing, and shoddy teaching. Once we cross the line that separates academic work from these other kinds, we are guilty both of practicing without a license and of defaulting on our professional responsibilities.

But isn't it our responsibility both as teachers and as citizens to instill democratic values in our students? Derek Bok thinks so and invokes studies that claim to demonstrate a cause and effect relationship between a college education and an active participation in the country's political life: "researchers have shown that college graduates are much more active civically and politically than those who have not attended college" (*Our Underachieving Colleges*). But this statistic proves nothing except what everyone knows: college graduates have more access to influential circles than do those without a college education. It does not prove that the inclination to participate in political life is produced by the *content* of a course or set of courses; a college degree may be a ticket of entry to the corridors of power; it does not follow, however, that the experience of earning it particularly fits one to walk those corridors successfully.

Even if there were a definite correlation between education and an active citizenry, that would not be a reason for teaching with the aim of fostering civic participation. Civic participation is a political rather than an academic goal. In a critique of my position, Elizabeth Kiss and Peter Euben ask, "Does a commitment to nurture core democratic principles on campus—to encourage and on occasion even to *force* students to engage as respectful equals with people of other races, cultures, religions, and ideologies—amount to an unjustifiable form of indoctrination?" The answer is "yes." Respecting those of other cultures, religions, and ideologies is a particular model of ethical behavior, but it would not be the preferred model of some libertarians, free-market economists, orthodox Jews, Amish, fundamentalist Christians, and members of the Aryan Nation, all of whom, the last time I looked, are American citizens and many of whom are college students. A university administration may believe with Kiss and Euben that "principles of equality and respect" form the core of democratic life, but if it pressures students to accept those principles as theirs, it is using the power it has to impose a moral vision on those who do not share it, and that is indoctrination if anything is. (It should go without saying that such an accusation would not apply to avowedly sectarian universities; indoctrination in a certain direction is quite properly their business.) As long as respect for the culture, religion, and ideology of the other is a contested ethic rather than a universal one, a university that requires it or attempts to inculcate it is engaged not in educational but in partisan behavior.

Bok is certainly aware that discussions of value harbor the danger of partisan indoctrination but believes that there is "a way of promoting certain values that does not amount to unacceptable indoctrination." But how does one tell the difference between acceptable and unacceptable indoctrination? The answer, it turns out, is that indoctrination is acceptable when it is performed in the service of the values favored by whomever is doing the indoctrinating. Bok's list of preferred values is a plausible one. He tells us that he favors honesty, the keeping of promises, and "more understanding of different races, backgrounds, and religions," goals, he says, "with which no reasonable person is likely to disagree." This is the oldest move in the liberal playbook—stigmatize in advance values antithetical to those liberalism professes and then dare anyone to disagree on pain of being declared unreasonable. (John Locke did it first in the *Letter Concerning Toleration*, 1689.) Bok attempts to blunt the coercive implications of what he urges by leaving room for student disagreement: "a student should always be free to question principles of behavior...no matter how correct they may seem." But rather than removing indoctrination from the classroom, this turns the classroom into a theater of competing indoctrinations. Permitting students to plump for the values they prefer as a counterweight to the values preferred by their professor sends the message that affirming (or rejecting) values is the business we are in, and that, as I've already said, is the wrong message. Preferring (or dis-preferring) values on the part of anyone, teacher or student, is just not a proper academic activity.

Paul Street, an urban researcher in Chicago, complains that by conceiving the academic task so narrowly, I turn professors into "good Germans, content to leave policy to those who are 'qualified' to conduct state affairs—people like George W. Bush and Donald Rumsfeld." Street's statement displays everything that is wrong about confusing teaching and political advocacy. Without bothering to argue the case, he assumes that George W. Bush and Donald Rumsfeld are today's fascist-militarists, and that it should be the business of every right-thinking (meaning left-thinking) academic to teach and write about the evil of their policies so that the emergence of a new Third Reich can be nipped in the bud.

Admittedly, many Americans and most academics in the humanities and social sciences share Street's political views, but does that mean that the educational experience of our students (many of whom hold opposing views) should be guided by them? Should the evil and perfidy of the Bush administration be the baseline assumption in the light of which history, literature, political theory, philosophy, and social science are taught? I think not (nor do I think that the virtue of the Bush administration should be the baseline assumption). In a classroom, the gathering of evidence on the way to reaching a conclusion is the prime academic activity. In Street's classroom, that activity would have been abandoned from the get-go; for him, the evidence is already in and the conclusion—a partisan conclusion—has been reached in advance.

Later in the piece Street identifies himself as "a former academic" who left the academy and now spends his time leading teach-ins and doing other politically oriented community work. He was right to leave; it was not his kind of thing. He was wrong to urge those who remain to perform in the classroom as he now does outside of it. Street can stand for all of those '60s activists who transferred their disappointed hopes for political revolution to higher education and the classroom. An entire generation has grown up believing that, as a provost at Brooklyn College put it, "Teaching is a political act." Only bad teaching is a political act.

Nor is teaching a political act in the milder sense of preparing students to assume their roles as citizens in a democratic society. Those who think that the fashioning of democratic citizens is an important educational goal are likely also to think that the business of education should be conducted in a democratic manner. They reason that because we live in a democratic society, the institutions we inhabit—and especially our institutions of higher education—should embody democratic principles.

But one need only recall the principles of democracy in order to see how poorly they fit the needs of an educational institution. Take the key principle of equality, for example. Under it, individual citizens have equal rights independently of differences in their intelligence, level of accomplishment, or age: seniority is a category of the census rather than the basis of privilege; anyone can say anything he or she likes (as long as it is not an incitement to violence, libel, or treason), and the state will levy no penalties even if what is said is unpopular or idiosyncratic in the extreme. Contrast that with what happens in college universities where the one man, one vote rule applies only if you've earned tenure, and seniority confers both privilege and power, and what you say or write can lead to your being denied promotion if your senior colleagues don't like it, and a thousand other things that come to mind the moment one starts to think of ways in which what goes on in the world of the academy is anything but democratic. It is not that there is a deliberate intention to be *un*democratic; it's just that being democratic rather than facilitating college business will often be seen to frustrate it by setting up obstacles in its way. While democratic governance is absolutely essential in a state dedicated to the idea that the people have the last word and the powerless can always vote out the powerful, democratic governance has a questionable relevance in a college or university where deans and provosts and presidents have the last word and can only be removed by someone above them in the hierarchy.

It is a question finally of what business we are in, and we are in the education business, not the democracy business. Democracy, we must remember, is a political not an educational project. It is a response to a problem formulated in the seventeenth century by the founders of Enlightenment Liberalism. The problem is that in any modern nation-state, citizens are committed to a bewildering array of belief systems, or as John Rawls calls them, "comprehensive doctrines." These are so disparate and so opposed to one another that if they are given their full sway in the public sphere, the result will be conflict, endless strife, and, eventually, civil war. The solution? Regard all citizens as free and equal political agents endowed with rights independently of what they happen to believe or who they happen to be, men, women, black, white, rich, poor, successful, or unsuccessful. The rights accorded every citizen are checks against abuses of power, and the most important check is provided by the ballot box, which allows the citizenry periodically to throw the rascals out.

The question is, what has this to do with scholarship and teaching, and the answer is, absolutely nothing. It is not the case that members of the academy are regarded as equal citizens despite differences in length of service, professional performance, research accomplishments, pedagogical effectiveness, etc. It is just these differences that make for *un*equal treatment, again not because administrators and promotion committees are being undemocratic, but because assessment and evaluation, not democracy, define their professional obligations. Moreover, evaluation and assessment are not tasks that can be distributed evenly across the population, both because those who are being evaluated cannot assume the role of judges in their own case, and because some in the population—students, staff, janitorial workers—lack the credentials that would make their evaluations meaningful and relevant. Even though certain elements of democratic procedures and principles may prove useful in an academic setting—note that "useful" is an administrative, not a moral, notion—democracy is not *generally* appropriate as a standard and benchmark in academic life.

## ACADEMIC FREEDOM

But what about the doctrine of academic freedom? Isn't it a quintessentially democratic idea and isn't it essential to the enterprise of higher education? Most faculty members certainly think so, for whenever they get into trouble for something they've said or want cover for something they're about to say or do, academic freedom is the first phrase on their lips. But more often than not, it is a phrase wrongly invoked in situations where it does not apply.

Consider the following example. In May 2003, journalist Chris Hedges was invited by President Paul Pribbenow to give the commencement speech at Rockford College. He spoke about Iraq and said among other things that the United States was an occupying force, and that "we will pay for this." Three minutes into his speech someone pulled the plug on the microphone; President Pribbenow spoke to the crowd and invoked academic freedom. Audience members shouted out protests. One of the soon-to-be graduates sitting on the stage got up and left. Hedges resumed speaking but cut his speech short and later said that he was surprised and saddened. "I had seen that in Belgrade, but I wasn't expecting to see it here."

What, then, are the First Amendment and academic freedom issues here? Exactly zero. Everyone did what he or she did freely. Pribbenow was free to invite Hedges. Hedges was free to say anything he liked, and even if Pribbenow had asked him to speak on a particular topic or avoid others, he would have been free to say no and decline the gig. The audience members were free to protest. The college would have been free to remove the protestors from the room, but there was no obligation to do so in the name of protecting the speaker's First Amendment rights. The soon-to-be graduate was free to leave the stage.

One might ask whether all these people *ought* to have done what they freely did, but that would be a question not of academic freedom but of appropriateness and judgment. Judgment was what President Pribbenow failed to exercise. He said that he wanted commencement "to be more than a pop speech," but could he not have anticipated that someone would have said what one member of the audience did say? "The day belongs to the students. It doesn't belong to a political view"? (Note that this doesn't mean that it was unconstitutional to give the platform over to a political view; it was just unwise.) Hedges said that this was not the first college at which he had given such a speech, but had he ever given one at a commencement? A commencement is a particular kind of occasion; it is, quite precisely, a ceremony, a formal rite of passage where etiquette and ritual are more important, and more appropriate, than profundity. Inviting controversial speakers to campus is certainly a good idea, but inviting controversial speakers to give a commencement address may not be. Pribbenow is reported to have decided that from now on he will seek speakers who would address matters important to people graduating from college. In short he will seek commencement speakers who will give a commencement speech. In the end, a lot of heat but little light; not many lessons learned—except the lesson that administrators should think things through before issuing invitations—and certainly no lesson about free speech or academic freedom.

Nor was either free speech or academic freedom the issue when the administration of Nova Southeastern University in Davie, Florida, invited author Salman Rushdie to be the commencement speaker at the Farquhar College of Arts and Sciences in 2006. Some student members of the International Muslim Association protested the invitation, presumably because they agreed with those who regarded Rushdie's 1988 novel *The Satanic Verses* as a blasphemy against Islam and the prophet Muhammad. Graduating senior Fahreen Paravez decided not to attend. "I was looking forward to my graduation," she said, but "when I found out that Salman Rushdie would be the speaker, I was appalled." Taken aback by the protest, NSU officials defended themselves by denying any malign intention—"Choosing Rushdie was not meant to insult anyone," said spokesperson Dean Don Rosenblum—and by pointing out that as a speaker Rushdie "fits well with NSU's yearlong study of Good and Evil." Apparently neither Rosenblum nor anyone else saw the tension between these two defenses: if Good and Evil is the theme, Rushdie must represent the former (you're not going to invite evil to be your speaker) and those who condemned him (and issued a fatwa against him) the latter; and if, as the protest indicated, there were graduating seniors who aligned themselves with the Ayotollah Khomeini and against Rushdie, they were sure to be insulted. It was not to the point to declare, as Rosenblum did, that Rushdie is "an outspoken advocate of freedom of expression, which is a critical core value of the university." To invoke freedom of expression as a core value is to elevate it above any and all of the sentiments that might be expressed; expression itself, rather than its content, becomes the cornerstone of your theology. But it is not, presumably, the cornerstone of the Muslim students' theology, and what they heard when the mantra of free speech was preached at them was another statement by the university that their beliefs—especially those that would lead to labeling some expressions blasphemous—are wrong.

The university tried to wriggle out of this one by turning the occasion into an educational experience. Professor Eileen Smith said, "I have great hopes that [Rushdie's] visit will inspire dialogue and a respectful, but lively, exchange of intellectual ideas." That sounds like what goes on, or should go on, in a classroom, but a graduation ceremony is not a class. The students do not come prepared to exchange intellectual ideas. They come prepared to be entertained, congratulated, and sent out into the world. They've already had four years of serious inquiry, and if that has been insufficient, 20 minutes more isn't going to be of much help. This day is reserved for lighter pleasures, and it is a commencement speaker's job to provide them. Rushdie's visit was trumpeted (in the college's announcement) as the "capstone" to a series of public lectures and classroom discussions of "tolerance, acceptance and social justice." One assumes that in the classrooms and at the public lectures vigorous participation was encouraged, and those who disagreed with the teacher or speaker could make their disagreement known in a context that had a place for it. But graduation speeches are not usually followed by question and answer periods or by a panel made up of persons representing opposing views. A graduation speech is a take it or leave it proposition and those who prefer to leave it must either walk out or resolve to stay home. Fahreen Parvez had it exactly right when she said, "If he were there for any other event, that would have been fine, because that's optional; but having him at graduation, it's not appropriate because that's for the families and the students." When you're the proud parent of a graduating son or daughter, the last thing you want to hear is something that will make you think. You want to hear something that will make you feel good. Professor Smith asserted that "the choice of Rushdie as speaker inspires questions, invites challenges and embodies larger issues." That's exactly the problem.

One year later, in 2007, it was the president of Columbia University, Lee Bollinger, who was seduced by the lure of larger issues. At the conclusion of his remarks to those assembled to hear and question President Mahmoud Ahmadinejad of Iran, Bollinger declared, "I am only a professor, who is also a university president, and today I feel all the weight of the modern civilized world yearning to express . . . revulsion at what you stand for."

By using the word "also" to introduce the fact of his administrative identity, Bollinger seemed to be saying, "I am a professor first and a university president second." But as everyone knows or should know, while university presidents may "also" be faculty members, both their obligations and their rights flow from their positions as administrators.

The obligation of a senior administrator is to conduct himself or herself in such a way as always to bring honor and credit to the institution he or she serves. Just what this general imperative requires will vary with the particular situations an administrator encounters, but at the very least we could say that an administrator who brings attention of an unwelcome kind to a university is probably not focusing on the job. He or she may be doing some other job—speaking truth to power, standing up for free speech, protesting against various forms of injustice—and those jobs may be well worth doing, but they belong to someone else.

So when President Bollinger said on another occasion, "I have free speech too," he was of course correct. He is free, like a faculty member, to say what he thinks about any issue when he is not in the classroom and bound by academic protocols; but unlike a faculty member, anything he says, even in extracurricular contexts, can be held against him by his employers. University administrators serve at will; and while, like other citizens, they enjoy freedom of speech, they do not enjoy immunity, as faculty members generally do, from the consequences—including possible dismissal—brought on by their having spoken freely.

Another way to put this is to say that when it comes to the activities of senior administrators, concepts like freedom of speech and academic freedom are not to the point. What is to the point are academic judgment and performance; those are the standards in relation to which Bollinger's performance should be assessed.

Now, it may be that he was speaking to constituencies within the university that were unhappy with some of his earlier actions in the ongoing controversy about the teaching practices of the Department of Middle East Asian Languages and Cultures. So, there may have been internal reasons—reasons not fully known to me and other commentators from the outside—that could account for his decision to take center stage and aggressively attack the Iranian president before he spoke.

Even so, as a general rule, what an administrator should do when a controversial speaker comes to campus is lower the stakes and minimize the importance of the occasion. Not minimize the importance of the issues, but minimize the role of the university, which is not a player on the world stage but (at most) a location where questions of international significance can be raised in an academic manner.

Bollinger was correct when he said in his remarks that it is appropriate "for the university to conduct such an event," but it is not appropriate for the university to be a front-and-center protagonist in the event. When Bollinger hurled his challenges at Ahmadinejad, he was saying explicitly, "here's where I stand on these issues," and therefore saying implicitly, "here's where Columbia University stands."

But Columbia does not, or at least should not, stand anywhere on the vexed issues of the day, and neither should its chief executive, at least publicly. After it was all over, Bollinger was applauded by some faculty members and students who are pro-Israel, and criticized by others who see Israel as the oppressor of the Palestinian people and lament the influence of what has been called the Israeli lobby. It would have been better if neither constituency were pleased or distressed by what he said, which means that it would have been better if he had said nothing, at least nothing substantive enough to amount to a position.

But how could Bollinger have managed to say nothing of substance once the invitation to Ahmadinejad had been extended (by a dean) and the predictable explosion of publicity had generated enormous expectations? Easy. Don't play to the expectations; instead, damp them down by turning the occasion into an academic rather than a political one. Bollinger could have begun by saying what was undoubtedly true, that the university had received many communications from faculty, students, and members of the public, all of whom posed questions they would have liked to put to the Iranian president. He could have said that he had selected a number of the most frequently asked questions and then posed them in a way that distanced him from their emotional force. "How would you reply to the contention that...?" "Many are worried that...." "Some have seen a contradiction between...." Exactly the same topics would have been brought up—Holocaust denial, nuclear proliferation, terrorism, Iraq—but in a spirit of inquiry rather than personal outrage. He could have presented himself as someone who was delivering the mail rather than as someone who was making the news.

It could be objected that if Bollinger had conducted himself in this manner, a great opportunity to stand up for what is right and say things that needed to be said would have been missed. But that is the kind of opportunity a university administrator would do well to miss. Leave the geopolitical pronouncements to the politicians whose job it is to make them and follow them up with actions. Remember always what a university is for—the transmission of knowledge and the conferring of analytical skills—and resist the temptation to inflate the importance of what goes on in its precincts. And don't think that everything that comes your way is a matter of free speech and academic freedom. These grand abstractions are invoked by academics at the slightest pretext, but in most situations in which administrators are required to act, they will only get in the way of seeing clearly what is and is not at stake.

The typical discussion of academic freedom will include a lot of talk about the value of unpopular ideas, the primacy of freedom, the nature of truth, and FDR's Four Freedoms. It is a phrase that *seems* resonant with large, philosophical implications, but it is really a narrow, modest thing: it is the freedom to do one's academic job without interference from external constituencies like legislators, boards of trustees, donors, and even parents. It is best thought of as a matter of guild protectionism, the name given to the desire of academics—and it is a desire hardly unique to them—to go about their business in ways defined by the nature and history of *their* enterprise rather than by some external constituency. Academic freedom, correctly (and modestly) understood, is not a challenge to the imperative always to academicize; it is the *name* of that imperative; it is the freedom to be an academic, which is, by definition, *not* the freedom to be anything and everything else. It doesn't mean don't interfere with me *whatever* I do—that would be a freedom no society that wished to remain a society could countenance—just don't interfere with me as I'm doing my job, so long as, in doing it, I am not breaking any laws.

In saying this I am merely rephrasing the American Association of University Professor's 1915 Declaration of Principles on Academic Freedom. After defining academic freedom as "freedom of inquiry and research, freedom of teaching within the university or college, and freedom of extramural utterance," the declaration adds that the claim to academic freedom can be asserted only by "those who carry on their work in the temper of the scientific inquirer" and never by those who would use it "for uncritical and intemperate partisanship." That statement is informed by the fear that external interests are always trying to take control of the academy. It used to be the church, the authors of the statement declare, but now it is "barbarous trustees" who constitute the danger. Whatever the danger, vigilance and resistance are necessary, and the first thing to be done, the statement goes on to say, is to make sure that our own house is clean and that we're doing the job we're supposed to do.

In short, one exercises academic freedom when determining for oneself (within the limits prescribed by departmental regulations and graduation requirements) what texts, assignments, and exam questions will best serve an academic purpose; one violates academic freedom by deciding to set aside academic purposes for others thought to be more noble or urgent.

Of course one is free to prefer other purposes to the purposes appropriate to the academy, but one is not free to employ the academy's machinery and resources in the service of those other purposes. If what you really want to do is preach, or organize political rallies, or work for world peace, or minister to the poor and homeless, or counsel troubled youths, you should either engage in those activities after hours and on weekends, or, if part-time is not enough time, you should resign from the academy, as Paul Street did, and take up work that speaks directly to the problems you feel compelled to address. Do not, however, hi-jack the academic enterprise and then justify what you've done by invoking academic freedom. The moment a teacher tries to promote a political or social agenda, mold the character of students, produce civic virtue, or institute a regime of tolerance, he or she has stepped away from the immanent rationality of the enterprise and performed an action in relation to which there is no academic freedom protection because there's nothing academic going on.

The limited freedom academics do enjoy follows from the task they perform. That task—extending the boundaries of received knowledge—does not have a pre-established goal; the open-endedness of intellectual inquiry demands a degree of flexibility not granted to the practitioners of other professions, who must be responsive to the customer, or to the bottom line, or to the electorate, or to the global economy. (That's why there's no such thing as "corporate manager freedom," or "shoe salesman freedom," or "dermatologist freedom.") If you think of academic freedom in this way—as a logical extension of a particular task and not as a free-standing value—you will be able to defend it both from those who see it as an unwarranted indulgence of pampered professors and from those pampered professors who would extend it into a general principle that allows them to say and do, or not do, whatever they like. To those who regard academic freedom as an unwarranted indulgence you can say, no, it's not an indulgence, it's a necessary condition for engaging in this enterprise, and if you want this enterprise to flourish, you must grant it; and to those professors who turn freedom into license by using the classroom as a partisan pulpit, or by teaching materials unrelated to the course description, or by coming to class unprepared or not at all, you can say, "look, it's freedom to do the job, not freedom to change it or shirk it."

## FREE SPEECH

But isn't academic freedom a subset of the overarching category of freedom of speech, a freedom accorded to all citizens by the Constitution?

Yes, of course professors have the right to say what they like *as citizens* (subject to the usual restrictions on libel, treason, and incitements to violence), but in their professional capacities the freedom they might claim is defined and limited by the nature of the task they are performing. My so-called free-speech rights will be very different depending, for example, on whether I am a fan at a baseball game or a nurse in an operating room. In the first context, my free-speech rights are pretty broad; I can yell any number of things, even abusive profane things, without being silenced, or arrested, or thrown out of the stadium. In the context of the operating room, however, my free-speech rights barely exist at all; if I decide, in the middle of a procedure, to advocate for a higher salary or better working conditions for nurses, I will have no First Amendment defense when I am hauled out of the room and later fired. The reason is that I would have been fired not because of the content of what I said, but because my words, whatever their content, were uttered in a setting that rendered them inappropriate and even dangerous.

Academic situations fall somewhere in between the base-ball stadium and the medical operating theater. In the context of the academy, where free speech is generally highly valued, you will have more or less free-speech rights depending on what you're doing and where you're doing it. If I am a student, and I begin to say something, and the teacher cuts me off and says that my point is beside the point he or she wishes to pursue, I have no free-speech recourse. On the other side, as an instructor I can conduct my class in any manner I like—lecture, discussion, group presentations—and I can assign whatever readings I judge to be relevant to the course's topic. Those are pedagogical choices, and I cannot be penalized for making them.

But if I harass students, or call them names, or make fun of their ethnicity, or if I use class time to rehearse my personal political views or attempt to win students over to them, I might well find myself in a disciplinary hearing, either because I am abusing my pedagogical authority or because I am turning the scene of instruction into a scene of indoctrination. What you are free to say in some venues you are not free to say in all venues, and your lack of freedom is not a First Amendment matter; it is a matter, rather, of the appropriateness or inappropriateness of certain kinds of speech relative to certain contexts of employment or social interaction.

Take the case of Ward Churchill. Churchill was a professor at the University of Colorado at Boulder, and he became famous, or rather infamous, because of an essay he wrote several years ago in which he went so far as to say that those who died in the September 11 attack on the World Trade Center were part of the military-industrialist machine that had produced the policies that had produced the hatred that eventually produced the terrible events of that day. When Churchill's remarks (which had appeared in an obscure journal) were unearthed and then publicized by Bill O'Reilly and other conservative commentators, legislators and ordinary citizens called for him to be fired. The argument for his dismissal was made on Chris Matthews's *Hardball*, by Kevin Lundberg, a state representative, who said that Churchill should be "held accountable" to "a common sense of values shared by the culture." Only in that way could he exhibit "professional integrity." But the reverse is true. If Churchill were to limit his conclusions to those already reached by the culture, he would throw his professional integrity out the window.

The fact that a large number of the officials and citizens of Colorado hated what Ward Churchill said is interesting sociologically. It is an answer to the (rather curious) question: what does Colorado think of Ward Churchill? But both the question and the answer (or any answer) have nothing to do with the question of his employment unless we want to go in the direction (symbolized for many by the old Soviet Union) of an academy whose research results are known in advance because they will always support the policies and reigning values of the state.

To its credit, the university's administration made the right call. Chancellor Philip DiStefano declared that "Professor

Churchill has the constitutional right to express his personal views." But DiStefano muddied the waters of the point he had just made when he added, "His essay on 9/11 has outraged and appalled us and the general public." This is at once confused and self-serving. One knows what DiStefano is up to: he is wrapping himself in the flag and mantra of strong First Amendment doctrine, that is, "I despise what you say, but I will defend to the death your right to say it." But it is not the job of a senior administrator either to approve or to disapprove of what a faculty member writes in a nonuniversity publication. It is his job to make the jurisdictional boundaries clear, to say something like "Mr. Churchill's remarks to the general public about matters of general political concern do not fall under the scope of the university's jurisdiction. He is of course free to make them, although one should not assume that in doing so he speaks for the university." Notice that this would stop short of either disavowing or embracing Churchill's remarks. The university can protect the integrity of its enterprise only if it disengages entirely from the landscape of political debate, if it says, in effect, we do academic, not political, business here. Simply by throwing in the egregious "has...appalled us," DiStefano has the university coming down on one side of a political question, and he also creates a First Amendment issue where there was none before.

DiStefano's statement may come back to haunt the university now that Churchill has been dismissed after a committee of scholars found him guilty of plagiarism and misrepresentation of his credentials. An appeal is in process, and one argument being made by Churchill's defenders is that the decision to scrutinize his record so closely was politically motivated, even if the ostensible reasons for firing him were appropriately pedagogical. It would not surprise me were Churchill's attorneys to cite what DiStefano said as evidence that he was being discriminated against because of the content of his constitutionally protected speech. After all, it could be argued, doesn't the fact that the chancellor of the university declared himself "appalled" by Churchill's ideas suggest that he had been disciplined because he holds those ideas?

In 2006, Kevin Barrett, a lecturer at the University of Wisconsin at Madison, took his place alongside Churchill as a college teacher whose views on 9/11 led politicians and ordinary citizens to demand that he be fired.

Mr. Barrett, who had a one-semester contract to teach a course titled "Islam: Religion and Culture," acknowledged on a radio talk show that he shared with students his conviction that the destruction of the World Trade Center was an inside job perpetrated by the American government. The predictable uproar ensued, and the equally predictable battle lines were drawn between those who disagree about what the doctrine of academic freedom does and does not allow.

Mr. Barrett's critics argued that academic freedom has limits and should not be invoked to justify the dissemination of lies and fantasies. Mr. Barrett's supporters (most of whom were not partisans of his conspiracy theory) insisted that it is the very point of an academic institution to entertain all points of view, however unpopular. This was the position taken by the university's provost, Patrick Farrell, when he ruled that Mr. Barrett would be retained: "We cannot allow political pressure from critics of unpopular ideas to inhibit the free exchange of ideas."

Both sides got it wrong. Each assumed that academic freedom is about ideas; one side thought that no idea should be ruled out in advance, while the other wanted to draw the line at propositions (like the denial of the Holocaust or the flatness of the world) considered by almost everyone to be crazy or dangerous.

But in fact, academic freedom has nothing to do with the expression of ideas. It is not a subset of the general freedom of Americans to say anything they like. Rather, academic freedom is the freedom of academics to *study* anything they like; the freedom, that is, to subject any body of material, however unpromising it might seem, to academic interrogation and analysis, to what I have called academicization. Any idea can be brought into a classroom if the point is to inquire into its structure, history, influence, etc. But no idea belongs in the classroom if the point of introducing it is to recruit students for or against a political agenda.

It is a matter of record that Mr. Barrett has a political agenda. He is a member of a group calling itself Scholars for 9/11 Truth, an organization with the declared aim of persuading Americans that the Bush administration "not only permitted 9/11 to happen but may even have orchestrated these events." The question is not, did he introduce his students to this account of the events of September 11, 2001? The question is, did he proselytize for it? Provost Farrell didn't quite see it that way, because he was too hung up on questions of content and balance. He thought that the important thing was to ensure a diversity of views in the classroom, and so he was reassured when Mr. Barrett promised to surround his "unconventional" ideas and "personal opinions" with readings "representing a variety of viewpoints."

But the number of viewpoints Mr. Barrett presented to his students was not the measure of his responsibility. There is, in fact, no academic requirement to include more than one view of an academic issue, although it is often pedagogically useful to do so. The true requirement is that no matter how many (or few) views are presented to the students, they should be offered as objects of analysis rather than as candidates for allegiance.

Thus the question Provost Farrell should have put to Mr. Barrett was not "Do you hold these views?" (he can hold any views he likes), or "Do you proclaim them in public?" (he has that right no less than the rest of us), or even "Do you surround them with the views of others?"

Rather, the question should have been: "Do you separate yourself from your partisan identity when you are in the employ of the citizens of Wisconsin and teach subject matter—whatever it is—rather than urge political action?" If the answer had been yes, allowing Mr. Barrett to remain in the classroom would have been warranted. If the answer had been no (or if a yes answer was followed by classroom behavior that contradicted it), he should have been shown the door. Not because he would have been teaching the "wrong" things, but because he would have abandoned teaching for indoctrination.

In neither the Churchill nor the Barrett case, then, is freedom of speech the real issue. But the temptation to view any issue as implicating one's free-speech rights is apparently irresistible. Indeed, the modern American version of crying wolf is crying First Amendment. If you want to burn a cross on a black family's lawn, or buy an election by contributing millions to a candidate, or vilify Jerry Falwell and his mother in a scurrilous "parody," and someone or some government agency tries to stop you, just yell "First Amendment rights" and you will stand a good chance of getting to do what you want to do. Frederick Schauer, a First Amendment scholar at Harvard University's Kennedy School, names this strategy "First Amendment opportunism."

Take the case of the editors of college newspapers who will always cry First Amendment when something they've published turns out to be the cause of outrage and controversy. In recent years, the offending piece or editorial or advertisement usually involves (what is at least perceived to be) an attack on Jews. A few years back, the *Daily Illini*, an independent student newspaper at the University of Illinois at Urbana-Champaign, printed a letter from a resident of Seattle with no university affiliation. The letter ran under the headline "Jews Manipulate America" and argued that because their true allegiance is to the state of Israel, the president should "separate Jews from all government advisory positions"; otherwise, the writer warned, "the Jews might face another Holocaust."

When the predictable firestorm of outrage erupted, the newspaper's editor responded by declaring, first, that "we are committed to giving all people a voice"; second, that, given this commitment, "we print the opinions of others with whom we do not agree"; third, that to do otherwise would involve the newspaper in the dangerous acts of "silencing" and "self-censorship"; and, fourth, that "what is hate speech to one member of a society is free speech to another."

Wrong four times.

I'll bet the *Daily Illini* is not committed to giving all people a voice—the KKK? man-boy love? advocates of slavery? would-be Unabombers? Nor do I believe that the editors sift through submissions looking for the ones they disagree with and then print those. No doubt they apply some principles of selection, asking questions like is it relevant, or is it timely, or does it get the facts right, or does it present a coherent argument? That is, they exercise judgment, which is quite a different thing from silencing or self-censorship. No one is silenced because a single outlet declines to publish him; silencing occurs when that outlet (or any other) is forbidden by the state to publish him on pain of legal sanction; and that is also what censorship is.

As for self-censoring, if it is anything, it is what we all do whenever we decide it would be better not to say something or cut a sentence that went just a little bit too far or leave a manuscript in the bottom drawer because it is not yet ready. Self-censorship, in short, is not a crime or a moral failing; it is a responsibility.

And, finally, whatever the merits of the argument by which all assertions are relativized—your hate speech is my free speech—this incident has nothing to do with either hate speech or free speech and everything to do with whether the editors are discharging or defaulting on their obligations when they foist them off on an inapplicable doctrine, saying in effect, "The First Amendment made us do it."

To be sure, the First Amendment protects unpopular as well as popular speech. But what it protects unpopular speech *from* is abridgement by the government of its free expression; it does not protect unpopular speech from being rejected by a newspaper, and it confers no positive obligation to give your pages over to unpopular speech, or popular speech, or any speech. There is no First Amendment issue here, just an issue of editorial judgment and the consequences of exercising it. You can print or say anything you like; but if the heat comes, it's yours, not the Constitution's.

In these controversies, student editors are sometimes portrayed, or portray themselves, as First Amendment heroes who bravely risk criticism and censure in order to uphold a cherished American value. But they are not heroes; they are merely confused and, in terms of their understanding of the doctrine they invoke, rather hapless.

Not as hapless, however, as the Harvard English department, which made a collective fool of itself three times when, in 2003, it invited, disinvited, and then reinvited poet Tom Paulin to be the Morris Gray Lecturer. Again the flash point was anti-Semitism. In his poetry and in public comments, Paulin had said that Israel had no right to exist, that settlers on the West Bank "should be shot dead," and that Israeli police and military forces were the equivalent of the

Nazi SS. When these and other statements came to light shortly before Paulin was to give his lecture, the department voted to rescind the invitation. When the inevitable cry of "censorship, censorship" was heard in the land, the department flip-flopped again, and a professor-spokesperson declared, "This was a clear affirmation that the department stood strongly by the First Amendment."

It was of course nothing of the kind; it was a transparent effort of a bunch that had already put its foot in its mouth twice to wriggle out of trouble and regain the moral high ground by striking the pose of First Amendment defender. But, in fact, the department and its members were not First Amendment defenders (a religion they converted to a little late), but serial bunglers.

What should they have done? Well, it depends on what they wanted to do. If they wanted to invite this particular poet because they admired his poetry, they had a perfect right to do so. If they were aware ahead of time of Paulin's public pronouncements, they could have chosen either to say something by way of explanation or to remain silent and let the event speak for itself; either course of action would have been at once defensible and productive of risk. If they knew nothing of Paulin's anti-Israel sentiments (difficult to believe of a gang of world-class researchers) but found out about them after the fact, they might have said, "Ooops, never mind" or toughed it out, again alternatives not without risk.

But at each stage, whatever they did or didn't do would have had no relationship whatsoever to any First Amendment right—Paulin had no right to be invited—or obligation—there was no obligation either to invite or to disinvite him, and certainly no obligation to reinvite him, unless you count the obligations imposed on yourself by a succession of ill-thought-through decisions. Whatever the successes or failures here, they were once again failures of judgment, not doctrine.

A failure of judgment was also at the heart of the Larry Summers saga, which ended with his resignation as the president of Harvard. Summers got into trouble when he speculated at an academic conference that the underrepresentation of women in the sciences might have a genetic basis.

The offended academic left saw Summers's remarks as an affront to its causes and as the latest chapter in the sad history of gender discrimination. The right (both inside and outside the academy) regarded the entire hullabaloo as an instance of political correctness run amok at the expense of Summers's First Amendment rights. And pundits on both sides thought that something deep about the nature of a university was at stake here. Brian McGrory, a *Boston Globe* columnist, achieved a new high in fatuousness, even in this rather dreary context, when he observed portentously, "I've always assumed that the strength of the academy is its ability to encourage difficult questions."

Well, that may be the strength of the academy, but it is not the strength sought by search committees when they interview candidates for senior administrative positions. No search committee asks, "Can we count on you to rile things up? Can we look forward to days of hostile press coverage? Can you give us a list of the constituencies you intend to offend?" Search committees do ask, "What is your experience with budgets?" and "What are your views on the place of intercollegiate athletics?" and "What will be your strategy for recruiting a world-class faculty?" and "How will you create a climate attractive to donors?"

Summers offered serial apologies for his comments but accompanied them with a defense that took them back. I was, he said, just being provocative. But being provocative is not in the job description. If straight-talking, with no concern for the fall-out that may follow, is what you like to do, you may not be cut out to be a university administrator. Not every virtue (if straight-talking is a virtue, and I have my doubts) is pertinent to every practice, and it is surely part of your responsibility to know what virtues are appropriate to the position you hold.

Stanley Kurtz opined in the *National Review* that Summers's critics had "turned him into a free-speech martyr," but that piece of alchemy could have been performed only if he had been prevented from speaking or punished by some state authority for the content of his words. In fact, he spoke freely, and if he suffered the consequences, they are not consequences from which the First Amendment protected him.

The First Amendment says that, in most circumstances, you can't be stopped from saying something and that, in many (but not all) circumstances, the content of what you say cannot be a reason for imprisoning you or firing you. But that doesn't mean that you get a free pass; you are not exempt from criticism; you are not exempt from public ridicule; you are not exempt from being voted out of your country club; and if what you have said causes enough of a ruckus, you are not exempt from being removed from your position, so long as the reason given for your removal is that your words have created conditions such that you can no longer do your job and not that somebody up there doesn't like their content. There is a big difference between "I don't like what that guy said, and I'm going to fire him" and "I don't like the effects brought about by what he said, and I'm going to fire him." The first raises constitutional issues (at least in some contexts); the second doesn't. It's just a judgment on job performance. The content of what Summers said was irrelevant to the only question that should been asked: is he discharging the duties and obligations of his office in a way that protects the reputation of the university and fosters its academic, political, and financial health? The Harvard Corporation asked that question, answered it in the negative, and came to a conclusion that had nothing whatsoever to do with Summers's free-speech rights.

The distinction between academic issues and free-speech issues seems to be a difficult one for both academics and those who criticize them. In 1997, the State University of New York at New Paltz sponsored a conference called "Revolting Behavior: The Challenges of Women's Sexual Freedom." Some called it borderline pornography and others celebrated it as an exercise in free speech. But what was interesting and depressing about the controversy was that both sides were indulging in the usual forms of bad faith, which they disguised by invoking sonorous abstractions.

Then governor George E. Pataki and the trustees who were egging him on displayed bad faith when they declared that the issue is scholarship and academic standards. No, the issue for them was that the scholarship represented in the conference's panels was scholarship they didn't like, in part because it didn't resemble the scholarship they encountered when they attended college a generation or two ago.

They didn't remember (and neither do I) any professor of theirs talking about body parts, excretory functions, the sex trade, dildos, bisexuality, transvestism, and lesbian pornography on the way to explicating Shakespeare or analyzing the political strategies of Queen Elizabeth I. But like it or not, that is the kind of talk and research being engaged in by many professors today.

Arguing against what is new in intellectual circles of course a respectable and necessary activity, but it is, or should be, an activity reserved for people who have read the relevant texts and are informed about the history and traditions of the disciplines. Governor Pataki and his political appointees were not those people.

Things weren't much better on the other side. If the critics of the New Paltz conference missed the mark (because they didn't know what the mark was and were not really interested in it anyway), the conference's defenders had their own way of obscuring what was really at stake.

To hear them talk, what was at stake was the abstract notion of free speech rather than the academic quality of what had actually been spoken. If it's speech and it takes place on a campus, they seemed to say, then it should be allowed to go on no matter what its content.

The trouble with this line of reasoning is that it short-circuits the consideration of the educational question—the question of what subjects and modes of instruction are educationally appropriate—and gives administrators reluctant to make decisions an all-purpose rationale for doing little and explaining nothing.

When SUNY trustee Candace de Russy complained that the conference "had absolutely nothing to do with the college's undergraduate mission," the college president, Roger W. Bowen, should have replied either, "Yes it does, and here's why," or, "You're right, and I made a mistake." Instead he went on about academic freedom and then added, as if to assure everyone that he knew trash when he saw it, that he "personally found several of their planned panel topics offensive."

"Offensive" is a word that allows Bowen to make a judgment and withdraw from it at the same time. He used it to avoid the real question: not whether the panels were offensive or inoffensive—neither quality is a reason for putting a panel on—but whether they were plausibly related to some sound educational purpose.

President Bowen was doing just what Governor Pataki did, but with an ACLU twist. Mr. Pataki said, I don't like it and therefore it doesn't belong on the campus. President Bowen said, I don't like it and therefore it does belong on the campus. The governor was trying to make campus life dance to the tune of his personal convictions. The college president was running away from his stated personal convictions—even those that relate to his office—in his eagerness to stand up for the First Amendment. One man was trying to do the other's job; the other had forgotten what his job is.

Both men were spouting the rhetoric demanded by their political situations, playing to constituencies—conservative Republicans and First Amendment zealots, respectively—that had very little stake in what actually happens at New Paltz and soon moved on to some other hot spot in the ongoing culture wars.

Meanwhile the news media, as usual, rode the story's extremes, and talk show panelists got to spend a couple of weeks hurling sound bites at one another—you say no tax dollars for whips, I say the First Amendment first, last, and always.

But that's not what it was really about. What it was really about was responsibility and the making of distinctions—distinctions about what a governor is supposed to do and what a college president is supposed to do, and the responsibility of one to keep his hands off the educational process and the responsibility of the other to be hands-on and not confuse genuine judgment with the invocation of some magic phrases.


## BENEFITS AND REWARDS

Those magic phrases—academic freedom and free speech—are what provide an alibi for professors who cannot tell the difference between a soapbox and a teacher's podium. It seems that every other day there is a report in the newspaper about teachers who inveigh against George Bush, or call

Israel the new Third Reich, or ridicule the claims and practices of organized religion, or champion the claims and practices of organized religion. These reports almost always provoke outrage and lead to demands by citizens and legislators that the offenders be removed from the classroom and taken off the payroll. Faculty associations and liberal watchdog groups (most of the activities found objectionable emanate from the left) respond by invoking academic freedom and free speech, and pretty soon the debate—predictable and dreary—becomes one about the nature of academic expression and the extent to which it does and does not have limits.

But this can of worms need never be opened if academics begin with the understanding that they are first and foremost academics and not wise men, gurus, and saviors, and that the only obligation to which they must be faithful is the obligation to present the material in the syllabus and introduce students to state-of-the-art methods of analysis. A teacher who understands this to be his obligation will never even be tempted to cross the line between pedagogy and activism. If everyone followed me in the resolve always to academicize, there would be no point to monitoring the political affiliation of faculty members, for that affiliation, whatever it might be, would not (except in the most attenuated way) be generating the analyses, descriptions, and data entries that serve as the basis of study and publication.

The advantage of this way of thinking about the issue is that it outflanks the sloganeering and posturing both sides indulge in: on the one hand, faculty members who shout "academic freedom" and mean by it an instructor's right to say or advocate anything at all with impunity; on the other hand, state legislators who shout "not on our dime" and mean by it that they can tell academics how to do their jobs.

# FIVE

# Don't Let Anyone
# Else Do Your Job

Of course, there's no shortage of people who will step in to do your job if you default on it. The corporate world looks to the university for its workforce. Parents want the university to pick up the baton they may have dropped. Students demand that the university support the political cause of the moment. Conservatives believe that the university should refurbish and preserve the traditions of the past. Liberals and progressives would like to see those same traditions dismantled and replaced by what they take to be better ones. Alumni wonder why the athletics teams aren't winning more. Politicians and trustees wonder why the professors aren't teaching more. Whether it is state legislators who want a say in hiring and course content, or donors who want to tell colleges how to spend the funds they provide, or parents who are disturbed when Dick and Jane bring home books about cross-dressing and gender change, or corporations that want new departments opened and others closed, or activist faculty who urge the administration to declare a position on the war in Iraq, there is no end of interests intent on deflecting the university from its search for truth and setting it on another path.

Each of these lobbies has its point, but it is not the university's point, which is, as I have said over and over again, to produce and disseminate (through teaching and publication) academic knowledge and to train those who will take up that task in the future.

But can the university defend the autonomy it claims (or should claim) from public pressures? Is that claim even coherent? Mark Taylor would say no. In a key sentence in the final chapter of his book *The Moment of Complexity* (2001), Taylor declares that "the university is not autonomous but is a thoroughly parasitic institution, which continually depends on the generosity of the host so many academics claim to reject." He continues: "The critical activities of the humanities, arts, and sciences are only possible if they are supported by the very economic interests their criticism so often calls into question." The standard rhetoric of the academy may be anti-market, but the "university and the people employed in it have always been *thoroughly* implicated in a market system."

As a description of the university's inevitable involvement with, and dependence on, the forces and investments of the larger society, this seems to me exactly right. But the prescriptive conclusion that Taylor draws from this description seems to me to be exactly wrong: let's stop pretending, he says, that we can operate in a splendid (but fictional) isolation from everything that enables us; let's accept the fact that we are in, and of, the market and "find new ways to turn market forces to [our] own advantage"; let's go beyond the kind of critical analysis that does little more than "promote organizations and institutions whose obsolescence is undeniable."

But if we are worried about obsolescence and the loss of relevance, the surest way to court both is to become so attuned to the interests and investments of other enterprises—the market, global politics, the information revolution—that we are finally indistinguishable from them. If there is nothing that sets us apart, if there is nothing distinctive about our task or the criteria for accomplishing it, if there is nothing that marks our work as ours and not everyone's, there will be no *particular* reason to support us by giving us a room (or a franchise) of our own. We will be exactly what Taylor suggests we are—a wholly owned (and disposable) subsidiary of something larger. Distinctiveness is a prerequisite both of our survival and of our flourishing. Without it we haven't got a prayer.

Taylor might reply that any distinctiveness we might claim would be illusory in light of the academy's radical dependence on others for financial support. No autonomy, no distinctiveness, no independent project. To argue in this way is to make what I call the "network" mistake—the mistake of thinking that because an entity or a practice has a form only in a network of relations, it is incoherent to speak of its properties, or of the boundaries that separate and distinguish it from other nodal points in the network. Since identity is network-dependent, the reasoning goes, nothing can be spoken of and examined as if it were freestanding and discrete.

The trouble with that reasoning is that it operates at a level of generality so high that you can't see the trees for the forest.

Yes, everything is finally interconnected and has a diacritical rather than a substantive existence (and is therefore, in some sense, not identical with itself), but it doesn't follow that there is nothing distinctive to say about "it," any more than it would follow that because the heart and lungs and the spinal cord are what they are by virtue of the system of which they are components, they perform no isolable functions, display no special characteristics, obey no special laws, and cannot be studied in their own right.

No one would say that about the parts of the body; nor should it be said of the university, which, despite the fact that the conditions of its possibility are exterior to it, does have an internal reality to which you must be attentive if you would hope to make observations that are relevant and (perhaps) helpful.

Indeed, if you do not attend to the internal perspective of a practice, you will be in danger of missing what is most crucial to its performance and you will ask it to do things appropriately done within the precincts of other practices, or you will complain that it does badly or minimally what it should not be doing at all. That is a risk more than courted by some of those who responded indignantly to John J. Mearsheimer's declaration (April 1998) that the University of Chicago "is a remarkably amoral institution" that makes "little effort to provide [students] with moral guidance." By that Mearsheimer does not mean that the university is immoral and gives bad counsel or that individual faculty members lack strong moral views; rather he means that the university gives no counsel, and that it is the professional, and in some sense moral, obligation of faculty members to check their moral commitments at the door.

The professional obligation is moral because it holds faculty members to the *particular* morality of the institution, the morality that comes along with its immanent rationality, which is the rationality of truth seeking, to which one cannot be faithful if one does not "condemn cheating, academic fraud, and plagiarism," all actions "antithetical to the search for truth."

To be sure, that is not the whole of morality—there are legions of moral issues left unaddressed—but it is, or should be, the whole of academic morality. Mearsheimer concedes that an academic morality, narrowly construed, does not meet all of the moral "demands of our society," but, he says, universities are not the institutions equipped or authorized to meet those demands: "providing moral guidance is no longer in their job description.... Religious institutions and families are expected to provide their members with explicit advice about moral virtue, but universities are not."

For the most part, those who take issue with Mearsheimer's statements fall into the everything-is-interconnected error. They reason that no human activity is without a moral dimension and add that this is particularly true of the activity of teaching. "I wonder," asks one such critic who responded to Mearsheimer's essay, "how we can expect our students to engage seriously and honestly in higher education itself if we studiously avoid all concern with moral education?"

And another interlocutor points out that in the humanities, the concerns of moral education are the explicit content of key texts: "How does [Mearsheimer] suppose anyone manages to teach Aristotle's *Ethics*, the Gospel according to St. Matthew, the works of Plato, Kant, and William James... without engaging students in genuine inquiry about what is moral and ethical behavior, and on what kind of persons they should become?"

But the fact that moral concerns turn up in the texts students study doesn't mean that what the students are learning about is morality. They are learning about the ways in which poets, philosophers, and political theorists structure their inquiries and reflections. Those inquiries and reflections will often begin and end with moral questions, but what makes those authors worth studying is not the answers they happen to give to those questions—you can find Plato and James compelling without either affirming or rejecting the morality they seem to be urging—but the verbal, architectonic, or

argumentative skills they display in the course of implement-
ing the intention to write a poem, or a piece of philosophy,
or a meditation on the nature of government.

The "genuine inquiry" in which students are (or should
be) engaged is not an inquiry about what kind of person they
should be but an inquiry about what kind of person Plato
or Hobbes or Rawls or Milton thought they should be,
and for what reasons, and with what poetic or philosophical force. The exam question is not, "If you were to find
yourself in such and such a situation, what should you do?"
The exam question is, "If you were to find yourself in such
and such a situation, what would Plato, Hobbes, Rawls,
and Kant tell you to do and what are the different assumptions and investments that would generate their different
recommendations?"

You can answer that question in a good academic fashion—
answer it, that is, as an academic question—without coming down on the side of any morality whatsoever, and no
instructor should penalize you because you stick to the
business at hand and decline the invitation—often proffered,
but always to be declined—to make the educational experience everything in general and nothing in particular.

I know that my strictures against university involvement in
political/moral matters can be read as an argument for passivity in the face of attacks on the academic enterprise. Elizabeth
Kiss and Peter Euben assert that when I say "aim low," I mean
"lay low." In fact I have repeatedly faulted senior administrators for laying low when it came time to defend their universities against funding cuts, legislative intrusions, and public
pressures (as applied, for example, by newspaper editorials
and radio talk shows). Indeed I have urged not passivity but
an aggressive and proactive stance that would have administrators playing offense rather than defense. I have made the
further point that universities argue from weakness when they

say to a legislature, or to a state board of higher education, or to a congressional committee, "See, what we do does in fact contribute to the state's prosperity, or to the community's cultural life, or to the production of a skilled workforce." All these claims may be true (although I doubt it), but to make them the basis of your case is to justify your enterprise in someone else's terms and play *his* game, and that, I contend, is to be passive in the defense of the institution's core values. Better, I counsel, to stand up for those values—for intellectual analysis of questions that may never have a definitive or even a useful answer, for research conducted just because researchers find certain problems interesting, for wrestling with puzzles only five hundred people in the whole world are eager to solve—and when those values are dismissed or scorned, challenge the scorner to exhibit even the slightest knowledge of what really goes on in the classroom or the laboratory; and when he or she is unable to do so, ask, "Is that the way you run *your* business, by pronouncing on matters of which you are wholly ignorant?" Now this advice may not be good advice—although the defensive strategies currently employed by administrators don't seem to work—but it is certainly not advice to be passive or lay low. Rather, it is advice to put your best food forward, which means, I believe, to put your *own* foot forward, and not someone else's.

This is a lesson forgotten or never learned by those administrators who performed badly in the wake of September 11. An example is the president of the University of South Florida, who agreed to the dismissal of a professor for having appeared on a television show and answered questions about statements he had made thirteen years previously. The reason given by the university for its action was that the hostile response to the professor's appearance disrupted day-to-day business (this is the "heckler's veto" argument, firmly rejected by a succession of Supreme Court decisions), but the real reason was that the president, rather than being true to her obligation to defend the academic enterprise, had given it over to the very political forces from which she should have protected it. She became the agent of those forces, and by doing their job, she defaulted on her own. You don't stand up for that enterprise by publicly judging (or, for that matter, approving) the constitutionally protected speech of those who look to you to be the spokesperson for, and the guarantor of, the integrity of their professional labors. In this case, the professor in question was later deported by the State Department after an investigation. But the fact that the president's suspicions of him proved out in the end does not mean that she was right to act on them before he was accorded due process.

## SHOULD UNIVERSITIES BE DEMOCRATIC?

"Due process" is a phrase in the lexicon of democracy, and my use of it might suggest that I am linking academic operations to democratic principles. But as I argued earlier, the question of how a democracy is to be administered and the question of how a university is to be governed are quite distinct, in part because university governance is a practical not a philosophical matter. That is to say, there is no *general* model of university governance. Each institution is differently situated with respect to its history, its mission, its size, the number and nature of its programs, its relationship to local, state, and national governments, its legal obligations and attendant dangers, its mechanisms of funding, and so on. Even something so apparently extraneous as the number of buildings and rooms on a campus can affect and perhaps undermine a grand proposal of governance reform. If revised regulations call for regular meetings and consultations but there are not enough spaces or hours in the day for either, the anticipated new utopia will quickly become the old dystopia, but even worse because expectations will have been provoked and then disappointed.

Nevertheless, while there may not be a general scheme of governance to which all should conform, there are general considerations that will be pertinent to any particular conversation. One might begin the conversation by clarifying some terms that are too often loosely employed. There is one term that rather than clarifying I would like to remove. That term is "stakeholder." Originally, the word referred to the third person who held the stakes—money, property, or some other good—for which two others were competing. But we now use the term in a much broader sense to mean all those who are (or might be) affected by an action taken by an organization or group.

Given a definition so capacious, who are the stakeholders in the world of higher education? Here is one answer offered in a white paper prepared for the ERIC Clearinghouse on Higher Education: "These stakeholders include higher education's associations, funding organizations, the U.S. Department of Education, related congressional committees, accrediting institutions, system-level offices, governors, state departments or boards of education, state legislatures, students, alumni, local community members, trustees, senior administrators, faculty leaders and presidents." The fact of a list as large as this one provokes protests on behalf of those who are not on it: staff, janitors, managers of student unions, community associations, professional sports teams, textbook publishers, book stores, vendors, caterers, neighborhood businesses, real estate developers, to name a few. Indeed, if the filter of inclusion is anyone who "might be affected," then there is no reason to exclude anyone, including newborn babies who certainly have a stake, albeit a long range one, in the enterprise.

Obviously a notion so diffuse will generate an equally diffuse model of governance, and it is no surprise that the authors (or are they stakeholders?) of the ERIC white paper end with this recommendation: "Perhaps a new governance model is in order for the university of the future—one that places the attitudes, values, and expectations of internal and external stakeholders at the center." In short, go out and ask everyone in sight how a university should be organized, and then build the answers, along with all the relevant "attitudes, values, and expectations," into a structure. Can anyone say "paralysis"? It has often been remarked that movement in a university is glacially slow, but glaciers will seem like rushing streams if no action can be taken that does not first satisfy the expectations of every so-called stakeholder.

It follows that the question of who are the stakeholders is an unprofitable one and is certainly not the right question to begin with. The right question is the one I've been asking on every page of this book. What's the nature of the academic enterprise? Once that question has been answered, the scope of its goals can be specified precisely, and it becomes possible to determine who should be given the responsibility for achieving them. The two answers often given to the question are: (1) We are a business. (2) We are in the business of democracy.

Much has been written about the inappositeness of thinking of the university as a business. Here is a representative statement by the Association of Governing Boards of Universities and Colleges:

> Nonprofit colleges and universities differ from businesses in many respects. They do not operate from a profit motive, and the "bottom lines" of colleges and universities are far more difficult to measure. They also differ from businesses in the sense that the processes of teaching, learning, and

research often are at least as important as "the product," as measured by the conferring of degrees or the publication of research results. And by virtue of their special mission and purpose in a pluralistic society, they have a tradition of participation in institutional governance that is less common in and less appropriate for business.

I find nothing here to disagree with, except, perhaps, for the gratuitous phrase "pluralistic society." I don't see that pluralism has anything to do with it. If, in fact, colleges and universities do have a core purpose, that purpose would have belonged to colleges and universities in the pre–World War II period when, while the society may have been pluralistic, the student population and the faculty certainly were not. I also am a bit bothered by the words "special mission." Every profession or practice has a special mission; if it did not, it would have no claim on our attention or support; if what it did were done elsewhere by others, there would be no reason for anyone to seek its services. I suspect that "special mission" carries a moral or even religious connotation: we are special because we live the life of the mind while others perform in less exalted ways. This form of academic smugness is always unattractive and spectacularly ineffective as a defense of the enterprise. Still, when all is said and done, the list of differences between the business world and the academic world offered here is pretty much on target. Higher education is just not in the same business as business.

There is nothing wrong, of course, with a university that is efficient, monitors its expenditures, and husbands its resources, so long as these and other bottom line strategies are understood to be in the service of a project they neither contain nor define. Things go wrong when the first question asked is "how much will it cost?" or "how much will it bring in?" rather than "what will it contribute?" or "how promising is it?"; for then decisions will be made without any reference to the reasons there are colleges and universities anyway. As Larry Gerber puts it in an essay in *Academe*: "advocates of a top-down management style who want to transform faculty from professionals into 'employees' and students into 'consumers' tend to see liberal education as a waste of time and resources, because they fail to see the immediate 'payoff' of the liberal and fine arts and because they are willing to allow the 'market' to determine what should and should not be taught." Once in place, Gerber continues, this market mentality spreads throughout the institution with unhappy results: "Encouraging students to view themselves primarily as consumers... too often results in pressures for lowering academic standards,... [since] student preferences to avoid courses with heavy reading assignments... may well result in administrative pressures on faculty to lower standards in order to maintain enrollments."

Gerber's antidote for these and other looming disasters is shared governance, which, he says, is more likely than the top-down corporate model of management "to foster the unimpeded pursuit and dissemination of knowledge that are necessary for the healthy development of society." But why should this be so? As long as the unimpeded pursuit of knowledge is acknowledged to be at the center of the university's mission, everyone in the chain of command, however it is configured, will have it in his or her mind to foster it. The values come first and if they are in place, they can be implemented by any organizational structure, although one can still argue about which organizational structure is best suited to the job.

Think, for example, about a department. Its structure might be autocratic, an old-fashioned head appointed for an indefinite term and responsible only to the dean, or it might be roughly egalitarian, the chair elected by the faculty and expected to carry out its wishes as they have been expressed in votes. There is much to be said about the advantages and disadvantages of these models, but good scholarship and good pedagogy can flourish or fail to flourish in either, and this remains true if we extrapolate from the department to the college and then to the university. The question of who does or does not participate in governance is logically independent of the question of whether the work being done is good or bad. Despite what Gerber would claim, the case for shared governance cannot rest on an intimate connection between its imperatives, which are philosophical and moral, and the imperatives of the academic project. What we do in the shop and how and by whom the shop is run are different matters. To conflate them is to turn an intellectual question—what is good scholarship and teaching?—into a political one—who shares in the power?

This is what Gerber does, and he does it because he makes the mistake—a natural and attractive one—of thinking that because we live in a democratic society, the institution we inhabit should embody democratic principles. The reasoning is that if democracy is good for the polity as a whole, it must be good for higher education. But what makes democracy work is an insistence on the priority of procedure over substance, or as Kant put it, the priority of the right over the good. Questions of the good are to be bracketed for the purposes of public life because to put them on the political table is to invite back the divisiveness the entire scheme is designed to outflank. In the words of legal philosopher Ronald Dworkin, the democratic liberal state is one that is, in its operations, "independent of any particular conception of the good life," which means, Thomas Nagel tells us, that in political deliberations "appeals to the truth" must be eschewed and we must learn to bracket our beliefs "whether moral, religious, or even historical and scientific" and regard them "simply as someone's beliefs rather than as truths."

However accurate this may be as a description of our civic duty, it does not describe our academic duty. An academic does not bracket or withdraw from his or her strong views about what is true; rather the task is to present, elaborate, and then defend those views by giving reasons and marshaling evidence. The task, in short, is not to be democratic, but to be rational. There may be times when the performance of rationality requires democratic process, but the two should not be identified. And it follows that if democratic imperatives are only instrumental and not central to academic purposes, the rationale for shared governance pretty much collapses; for in its strongest form, with its insistence that the franchise be extended as widely as possible, it is indistinguishable from representative democracy and therefore from the stakeholder model, in which, because everyone is in charge, no one is in charge. The question of who does and does not share in governance is not a philosophical one to be answered by some political theory; you answer it by identifying the task and surveying the resources and obstacles attendant upon it. Then you are in the position to figure out who should be given the responsibility for getting the job done, a matter not of grand moral pronouncements, but of good management.

Indeed, shared governance is not a style of management, but an impediment to management for reasons elaborated by John Lombardi, president of the University of Massachusetts at Amherst. "Universities for the most part do not have management; they have governance," which Lombardi defines as "the political process that balances the various competing interests of an institution through a complicated and lengthy process." Governance of the shared kind has the tendency to substitute process for action, and that, says Lombardi, means that action will be endlessly deferred.

> To improve, the university must have management. It must have direction. The institution must consult…must listen, and it must respond to…advice from its many constituencies, but it must nonetheless act, and often it must act without complete consensus.

The difference between management and shared governance is that management is by and large aware of its instrumental status—it does not define the job, but helps to get it done—while those who preach the gospel of shared governance tend to think of it as another name for the job, or, at the very least, as the model of organization that belongs naturally to the job. That is why advocates of shared governance are likely to be unimpressed when Lombardi complains that this politically inspired concept, when put into operation, prevents the organization from moving forward. Exactly right, the self-righteous faculty member will reply, and it's a good thing too, because the organization—meaning the senior administration from the office of the dean to the president to the board of trustees—is a structure of power, and it is one's positive duty to frustrate its working.

Here is still another way in which academic life differs from the life of business. In the business world, those at the top of the organizational hierarchy are regarded (not only by themselves but by others lower on the food chain) as the key players and as the ones best positioned and equipped to make the important decisions. In the academic world, by contrast, faculty members regard senior administrators with contempt, believing them to be either burnt-out scholars or failed scholars whose flame was never ignited in the first place. The organizational chart of a university may suggest that authority rests with the administrators, who, as the management class, set the standards to which faculty, the labor class, must conform. But faculty are reluctant to think of themselves as labor (hence the resistance to unionization) and are convinced—a conviction that seems to be issued to them along with the Ph.D.—that authority really rests with them and that the hierarchy announced in the organizational chart is a fiction they are in no way obliged to respect. I once explained this to someone who asked, "Well, if they think that, why don't they assume the positions in the hierarchy themselves?" The answer, of course, is that they would believe that any such grubbing after administrative power is beneath them; they, after all, inhabit the life of the mind, and because they inhabit the life of the mind, they have a right not to be coerced by bean-counters in three-piece suits and power dresses and certainly should not aspire to be like them.

This sense of entitlement—we are the real center of the enterprise; deans, provosts, and presidents only serve us—comes easily to those who assimilate the university to the model of democracy, a model in which power is assumed to be always corrupt and always in need of rebuke and check by those of purer heart and mind. If you are a dean or a provost, you might be understandably reluctant to share governance with a crew like that; for you would know that they would come to the task with a set of attitudes that, rather than facilitating the smooth running of the university's machinery, is likely to put a spanner in the works, and is likely to do so for what will seem to them to be *moral* reasons: we are doing no more than asserting our intellectual or academic freedom, which in some cases turns out to be not only freedom from external intrusions into the everyday business of workplace, but freedom from the everyday obligations of the work place. Why should I teach three days a week? Why should I teach this subject just because my chair told me to? Why must I post office hours and keep them? Why can't I hold class at my house or at the beach?

As someone who has been there, I have a great deal of sympathy with Harry Haynsworth, retired president and dean, William Mitchell College of Law, who, after fourteen years of wrestling with the appropriate division of governance responsibilities between the faculty and the administration, reported that "in recent years I have consciously tried to limit the number of issues that will ultimately come before the entire faculty for its approval." Haynsworth knows that he is out of step with conventional wisdom. "I have been told more than once that my views on faculty governance boundaries are much too narrow and not in accordance with the traditions of academia and the practices of most faculties." He continues to believe, however, that his "basic convictions are sound and are supported by respectable authority."

His convictions are also supported by what is practiced in most colleges and universities. In very few institutions is governance really shared, even when official documents declare that it is. Here, for example, is a sentence from the "Guidelines for Shared Governance" at the University of Arizona: "Students, classified staff and professional personnel should participate in the shared governance process where appropriate and in a fitting manner." And who gets to decide what is fitting and appropriate? The answer is given by another sentence: "The Task Force recommends that the President commits to and takes a leadership role in smoothing the way for shared governance at all levels." In the final document, approved by the faculty senate in April 2005, the true and sensible meaning of shared governance becomes clearer:

> the success of the University and the positive morale of the faculty and administration are dependent upon continued use of the collective intelligence of the university

community. . . . This requires extensive sharing of information and a shared understanding that faculty representatives
and administrators strive always for informed mutual support through shared governance dialogue.

"Shared governance dialogue" is a phrase I almost like
despite its clunkiness because it gets close to telling the
truth. What is, in fact, important to morale and therefore to
the success of the university is *talk* about shared governance,
for what really ought to be shared is information. Faculties are not distressed because they have too small a portion
of the administrative task—one provost told me recently,
"when they ask for money and governance I always give
them governance because they soon tire of using it"—but
because they only learn about administrative decisions after
they have been made. It is the withholding of information,
not of responsibility, that leaves faculty members feeling left
out, taken for granted, and generally disrespected. For some
reason, the hoarding of information is a reflex action on
the part of most administrations. The thinking may be to
control the situation by controlling the flow of information;
but the truth is that in the absence of information, rumor,
conspiracy theories, and ultimately real conspiracies rush in
to fill the space that would not even have been there if full
disclosure had been the policy. Tell them everything: share
every piece of information you have the moment you have
it, and they will be quite happy to leave the governance
to you, especially if as you distribute the information you
invite them to talk about the issues it raises. They get to feel
that they are a part of what is going on; you get the benefit
of hearing their views without having to promise that you
will act in accordance with them.

This is also the way to deal with students who always
want to have a say in everything. And while students may

be excused for wanting to play a role not properly theirs, administrators should know better and should always remember the differences between tasks and the capabilities necessary to perform them. I'm not saying don't consult with students. Consult with everyone, but don't confuse consulting with the sharing of the franchise. Student evaluation of teaching is bad enough (I lost that battle over forty years ago), but at least those forms are sometimes read with caution by those who know what they are and what they are not. No such caution, or knowledge, or competence attends the performance of students who are allowed by some misguided administration to vote or serve on search committees. They will influence the process according to their interests (what else would you expect them to do?), but their interests are short term and only obliquely related to the interests of those who will spend much of their lives in the institution.

If students should be kept to the side of academic business because they haven't the qualifications for the job, the same is true for trustees, donors, politicians, parents, and concerned members of the general public, all of whom have lots of ideas that should be politely listened to and then filed away under "not to the academic point." It's not that these people aren't smart; they're usually very smart in their own lines of work. It's just that most of the time the models and examples they urge on you presuppose conditions and criteria that have nothing to do with the conditions and criteria of the academy.

## THE CULTURE WARS

Invoking criteria that are beside the point of the academic enterprise is what routinely happens in the culture wars, now in their third decade. Who is winning?

If victory for the right meant turning back or retarding the growth of programs like women's studies, African American studies, Chicano studies, Latino studies, cultural studies, gay and lesbian (and now transgender) studies, postmodern studies, and poststructuralist theory, then the left is winning big time, for these programs flourish (especially among the young) and are the source of much of the intellectual energy in the liberal arts.

But if the palm is to be awarded to the party that persuaded the American public to adopt its characterization of the academy, the right wins hands down, for it is now generally believed that our colleges and universities are hotbeds of radicalism and pedagogical irresponsibility where dollars are wasted, nonsense is propagated, students are indoctrinated, religion is disrespected, and patriotism is scorned.

In short, the left may have won the curricular battle, but the right won the public-relations war. The right did this in the old-fashioned way, by mastering the ancient art of rhetoric and spinning a vocabulary that, once established in the public mind, performed the work of argument all by itself. The master stroke, of course, was the appropriation from the left (where it had been used with a certain self-directed irony) of the phrase "political correctness," which in fairly short order became capitalized and transformed from an accusation to the name of a program supposedly being carried out by the very persons who were the accusation's object. That is, those who cried "political correctness" invented an entity about which they could then immediately complain. This was genius.

Now they're doing it again, this time by taking a phrase that seems positively benign and even progressive (in a fuzzy-left way) and employing it as the Trojan horse of a dark design. That phrase is "intellectual diversity," and the vehicle that is bringing it to the streets and coffee shops of your home town is David Horowitz's Academic Bill of Rights, which has been the basis of legislation introduced in Congress, has stirred some interest in a number of state legislatures, and has been the subject of editorials (both pro and con) in leading newspapers.

Opponents of the Academic Bill of Rights contend that despite disclaimers of any political intention and an explicit rejection of quotas, the underlying agenda is the decidedly political one of forcing colleges and universities to hire conservative professors in order to assure ideological balance.

Horowitz replies (in print and conversation) that he has no desire to impose ideological criteria on the operations of the academy; he does not favor, he tells me, legislation that would have political bodies taking over the responsibility of making curricular and hiring decisions. His hope, he insists, is that colleges and universities will reform themselves, and he offers the Academic Bill of Rights (which is the product of consultation with academics of various persuasions) as a convenient base-line template to which they might refer for guidance.

For the record, and as one of those with whom he has consulted, I believe him, and I believe him, in part, because much of the Academic Bill of Rights is as apolitical and principled as he says it is. It begins by announcing that "the central purposes of a University are the pursuit of truth, the discovery of new knowledge through scholarship and research, the study and reasoned criticism of intellectual and cultural traditions . . . and the transmission of knowledge and learning to a society at large." (I shall return to the clause deleted by my ellipsis.)

The bill goes on to define academic freedom as the policy of "protecting the intellectual independence of professors, researchers and students in the pursuit of knowledge and the expression of ideas from interference by legislators or authorities within the institution itself."

In short, "no political, ideological or religious orthodoxy will be imposed on professors." Nor shall a legislature "impose any orthodoxy through its control of the university budget," and "no faculty shall be hired or fired or denied promotion or tenure on the basis of his or her political or religious beliefs." The document ends by declaring that academic institutions "should maintain a posture of organizational neutrality with respect to the substantive disagreements that divide researchers on questions within, or outside, their fields of inquiry."

It's hard to see how anyone who believes (as I do) that academic work is distinctive in its aims and goals and that its distinctiveness must be protected from political pressures (either external or internal) could find anything to disagree with here. Everything follows from the statement that the pursuit of truth is a—I would say, *the*—central purpose of the university. For the serious embrace of that purpose precludes deciding what the truth is in advance, or ruling out certain accounts of the truth before they have been given a hearing, or making evaluations of those accounts turn on the known or suspected political affiliations of those who present them.

But it is precisely because the pursuit of truth is the cardinal value of the academy that the value (if it is one) of intellectual diversity should be rejected.

The notion first turns up, though not by name, in the clause I elided where Horowitz lists among the purposes of a university "the teaching and general development of students to help them become creative individuals and productive citizens of a pluralistic society."

Teaching, yes—it is my job, as I have said repeatedly, to introduce students to new materials and equip them with new skills; but I haven't the slightest idea of how to help students become creative individuals. And it is decidedly not

my job to produce citizens for a pluralistic society or for any
other. Citizen building is a legitimate democratic activity,
but it is not an academic activity. To be sure, some of what
happens in the classroom may play a part in the fashioning
of a citizen, but that is neither something you can count
on—there is no accounting for what a student will make
of something you say or assign—nor something you should
aim for. As admirable a goal as it may be, fashioning citizens
for a pluralistic society has nothing to do with the pursuit
of truth.

For Horowitz, the link between the two is to be found
in the idea of pluralism: given the "unsettled character of all
human knowledge" and the fact (which is a fact) "that there
is no humanly accessible truth that is not in principle open
to challenge," it follows, he thinks, that students being prepared to live in a pluralistic society should receive an education in pluralism; and it follows further, he says, that it is
the obligation of teachers and administrators "to promote
intellectual pluralism" and thereby "protect the principle of
intellectual diversity."

But it is a mistake to go from the general assertion that
no humanly accessible truth is invulnerable to challenge to
the conclusion that therefore challenges must always be provided. That is to confuse a theory of truth with its pursuit
and to exchange the goal of reaching it for a resolution to
keep the question of it always open.

While questions of truth may be generally open, the
truth of academic matters is not general but local; questions
are posed and often they do have answers that can be established with certainty; and even if that certainty can theoreti-
cally be upset—one cannot rule out the future emergence
of new evidence—that theoretical possibility carries with
it no methodological obligation. That is, it does not mandate intellectual diversity, a condition that may attend some

moments in the pursuit of truth when there is as yet no clear path, but not a condition one must actively seek or protect.

To put it simply, intellectual diversity is not a stand-alone academic value, no more than is free speech; either can be a help in the pursuit of truth, but neither should be identified with it; the (occasional) means should not be confused with the end.

Now if intellectual diversity is not an academic value, adherence to it as an end in itself will not further an academic goal; but it will further some goal, and that goal will be political. It will be part of an effort to alter the academy so that it becomes an extension of some partisan vision of the way the world should be.

Such an effort will not be a perversion of intellectual diversity; intellectual diversity as a prime academic goal is already a perversion, and its transformation into a political agenda, despite Horowitz's protestations and wishes to the contrary, is inevitable and assured. It is just a matter of which party seizes it and makes it its own.

For a while (ever since the *Bakke* decision), it was the left that flew the diversity banner and put it to work in the service of affirmative action, speech codes, hostile-environment regulations, minority hiring, and more. Now it is the right's turn, and Horowitz himself has mapped out the strategy and laid bare the motives:

> I encourage [students] to use the language that the left has deployed so effectively on behalf of its own agendas. Radical professors have created a "hostile learning" environment for conservative students. There is a lack of "intellectual diversity" on college faculties and in academic classrooms. The conservative viewpoint is "under-represented" in the curriculum and on its reading lists. The university should be an "inclusive" and intellectually "diverse" community. (April 2003)

It is obvious that for Horowitz these are debating points designed to hoist the left by its own petard; but the trouble with debating points is that they can't be kept in bounds. Someone is going to take them seriously and advocate actions that Horowitz would probably not endorse.

Someone is going to say, let's monitor those lefty professors and keep tabs on what they're saying; and while we're at it, let's withhold federal funds from programs that do not display "ideological balance"; and let's demand that academic institutions demonstrate a commitment to hiring conservatives; and let's make sure that the material our students read is pro-American and free of the taint of relativism; and let's publish the names of those who do not comply.

This is not a hypothetical list; it is a list of actions already being taken. In fact, it is a list one could pretty much glean from the Web site of Colorado state senator John K. Andrews Jr., a site on which the Academic Bill of Rights is invoked frequently.

Andrews, like everyone else doing the intellectual diversity dance, insists that he opposes "any sort of quotas, mandated hiring or litmus test"; but then he turns around and sends a letter to Colorado's universities asking them to explain how they promote "intellectual diversity." If he doesn't like the answers he gets, he promises to sponsor legislation to "ensure academic freedom."

Anne Neal, of the Lynne Cheney–inspired American Council of Trustees and Alumni, plays the same double game in a piece entitled "Intellectual Diversity Endangered." First she stands up for the value of academic freedom ("no more important value to the life of the mind"), but then she urges university trustees to see to it "that all faculty . . . present points of view other than their own in a balanced way" (something you might want to do but shouldn't have to do), and to "insist that their institutions offer broad-based survey courses," and "to monitor tenure decisions" for instances of "political discrimination," and to "conduct intellectual diversity reviews and to make the results public." In short, she urges trustees to take over the university and conform its operations to neoconservative imperatives.

The irony is that while intellectual diversity is urged as a way of fighting the politicization of the university, it *is* the politicization of the university, for it requires the faculty to display the same proportion of Democrats and Republicans as is found in the general population, which makes about as much *academic* sense as requiring the same proportion in the corporate boardroom or on the roster of the Boston Red Sox would make economic or athletic sense.

As one example of the damage that can be done under the banner of intellectual diversity, consider Florida House Bill 837 introduced a couple of years ago by state representative Dennis Baxley. In that bill we read that students have a right "to take reasoned exception to the data and views offered in any course of study," that students have a right to the introduction in a course of "a broad range of serious scholarly opinion," and that "the fostering of a plurality of serious scholarly methodologies and perspectives should be a significant institutional purpose."

Sounds innocuous, but the bland words barely mask an effort to take instruction out of the hands of instructors by holding them to curricular quotas and threatening them with student lawsuits if they fail to comply. First of all, students do not have any rights except the right to competent instruction, and one part of being a competent instructor is the ability (and responsibility) to make judicious—not legislatively imposed—decisions about what materials and approaches are to be taught. The decision to include or exclude a particular approach should depend on the instructor's academic judgment and not on the need to display a mandated balance by some measure that is never announced, but is, we know, the measure of how many so-called conservative voices and approaches are represented. You shouldn't be reduced to saying, I guess I'll have to look for one of these because I don't have enough of them on the syllabus. You should instead be asking is this text or methodology really important and worth devoting precious class time to?

Should teachers really be forced to introduce a perspective just because it is out there and is supported by a group of true believers? "Yes" would be the answer of representative Baxley, who when asked for an example of the kind of professorial behavior that might lead to a grievance cited the refusal of biology teachers to discuss Intelligent Design when students raise questions about it. The overwhelming professional and disciplinary consensus is that the theory of Intelligent Design is not the answer to any scientific question and that therefore study of it should take place in cultural studies courses. The overriding of that professional consensus proposed by Mr. Baxley is a naked example of the political agenda that will always be found just below the surface of apparently benign slogans like intellectual diversity, pluralism, and balance, all bad ideas because they substitute political goals for academic ones.

—⁂—

It is more than a little ironic that these bad ideas—turned to political advantage by the right—often have their home on the left. When, for example, George W. Bush said that evolution and Intelligent Design should be taught side by side so that students "can understand what the debate is about," he probably didn't know that he was signing on to the wisdom of Gerald Graff, a professor of English at the University of Illinois, Chicago, and founder of Teachers for a Democratic Culture, an organization dedicated to "combating conservative misrepresentations" of what goes on in college classrooms. Graff and Intelligent Design are now a couple on the Internet even though he had never written a word on the subject until he wrote in protest against his having been "hijacked by the Christian Right." He has, however, written many words urging college instructors to "teach the conflicts" that typically grow up around an issue so that students will learn that knowledge is neither inertly given nor a matter of personal opinion ("I've got mine and you've got yours"), but is established in the crucible of controversy. Although Graff makes his case for teaching the controversies in a book titled *Beyond the Culture Wars* (he wants partisan posturing to be replaced by rational debate), the culture wars have now appropriated his thesis and made it into a weapon in the arsenal of the Intelligent Design warriors. From Bush on down to every foot soldier in the army, "teach the controversy" is the battle cry.

It is an effective one, for it takes the focus away from the scientific credibility of Intelligent Design—away from the question, "Why should it be taught in a biology class?"—and puts it instead on the more abstract issue of freedom and openness of inquiry. Rather than saying, "we're right and the other guys are wrong and here are the scientific reasons," they say things like "questions of right and wrong must always be left open," "every idea should at least get a hearing," "unpopular or minority views should be represented and not suppressed," and "what currently counts as knowledge should always be suspect because it will typically reflect the interests and preferences of those in power." This last bit is standard vulgar postmodernism of the kind one gets by reading a page or two of some French theorist, and what is interesting about its appearance in these debates is that those who mouth it don't believe it for a minute; it's just a matter of political tactics.

Philip E. Johnson, a leading Intelligent Design advocate, is quite forthright about this. "I'm no postmodernist," he declares in an interview, but "I've learned a lot" from reading them. What he's learned, he reports, is how to talk about "hidden assumptions" and "power relationships" and how to use those concepts to cast doubt on the authority of "science educators" and other purveyors of the reigning orthodoxy. My views, he says, "are considered outlandish in the academic world," but the strategy he borrows from the postmodernists—the strategy of claiming to have been marginalized by the powers-that-be—is, he boasts, "dead bang mainstream academia these days."

This is nothing if not clever, but it is also disingenuous and a bit dishonest because it involves hitching your wagon to a set of ideas you really despise. In an academy where talk of marginalization and hegemonic exclusion is routine, Johnson and his friends can use that talk (in which they have no real stake) to gain a hearing for ideas that have failed to make their way in the usual give-and-take of the academic debates Graff celebrates. While in Graff's book "teach the controversies" is a serious answer to a serious question—how can we make students aware of the underlying issues that structure academic discourse?—in the work of Johnson and other Intelligent Design proponents, "teach the controversies" is the answer to no question. Instead it is a wedge for prying open the doors of a world to which they have been denied access by gatekeepers—individual scientists, departments of biology, professional associations, editors of learned journals—who have found what they say unpersuasive and beside the scientific point. They say "teach the controversy," but they mean, "let us into the conversation even though the almost universal judgment of authoritative researchers is that we have nothing relevant to contribute."

They get away with this (or at least try to) by lowering the stakes in the guise of upping them. They appeal to a higher value—the value of fairness or the value of controversy as a moral good in and of itself—and thereby avoid questions about the qualifications necessary to be legitimate competitors in the intellectual arena. They insulate their arguments from detailed objections by attaching them to an abstract value, which is then piously affirmed. In the light of this value—fairness and/or free inquiry—their claims shed their specificity and become indistinguishable from the claims of their opponents. They ask, "In a democratic discussion, shouldn't every voice be heard?" rather than asking, "Which voices have earned (through the usual mechanisms of validation) the right to be heard?"

The same leveling effect is achieved when Intelligent Designers invoke a long view of history. Isn't it the case, they ask, that only a few decades ago it was evolutionary theory that was kept out of some classrooms in this country? That proved to be an error, they point out, and isn't it possible that someday the present policy of refusing to teach Intelligent Design in science classes will be thought to have been an error too? After all, haven't many once discredited theories and avenues of research been accepted by a later generation of scholars? And doesn't history show us that apparently settled wisdom is often kept in place by those whose careers are invested in it?

The answer to all these questions is "Yes," but the yes carries with it no methodological implications because the long view of history does not provide any answers to questions posed at a particular moment in time. All it does is tell you how some of those answers fared. The fact that some of them have not fared well does not tell you how to proceed with a new question (like "has evolutionary biology led to advances in understanding and research?") that arises in the present. "Expert judgment" as a category of validation is not discredited generally because it has occasionally turned out to be wrong. You have to go with the evidence you have, even if it is true that the evidence you have may be overtaken in the long run. It would not be a method at all—it would be a bizarre non sequitur—to say, "Given that we don't know now what might turn up in the distant future, let's systematically distrust everything that now appears to us to be sound and true."

Unfortunately (or fortunately for the Intelligent Design agenda), this is precisely what is said by some postmodernists and multiculturalists, and in saying it they are merely drawing out the implications of one strain of liberalism, the strain that finds its source in John Stuart Mill's insistence (in *On Liberty*) that knowledge should never be allowed to settle and congeal. This has also been the view of First Amendment doctrine, at least since *New York Times v. Sullivan* (1964), a case in which the values of truth and accuracy are subordinated to the supposedly greater value of "uninhibited, robust, and wide-open" discussion. In its opinion the Court blurs the distinction between true and false statements by recharacterizing the latter (in a footnote that cites Mill) as a "valuable contribution to the public debate," thus paving the way for those who, like the advocates of Intelligent Design, assert that their views deserve to be considered (and taught) even when—especially when—the vast majority of authorities in the field have declared them to be without scientific merit. It is an assertion that liberals by and large resist when the message asking for a place at the table is racist or sexist, but it is a logical consequence of liberalism's privileging of tolerance and multivocality over judgment.

Liberalism privileges tolerance because it is committed to fallibilism, the idea that our opinions about the world, derived as they are from the local, limited perspectives in which we necessarily live, are likely to be in error even when, again especially when, we are wholly committed to them. Because this mistake is natural to us, because the beliefs we acquire always seem to us to be perspicuous and indubitable, it is necessary, liberalism tells us, to put obstacles in the way of our assenting too easily to what are finally only our opinions.

By rooting itself in fallibilism, liberalism casts a prospective shadow on any determination of right and wrong and makes it difficult to justify the exclusion from the conversation of any point of view. A reasonable methodological caution—don't assume that your convictions are incapable of being proven wrong—is pressed until it becomes a metaphysical imperative—always assume that whatever "authoritative selection" has delivered is the result of a politically inspired act of exclusion. This transformation of a "check and balance" into a hermeneutics of suspicion was always implicit in liberalism's logic, but it achieves fully realized form in those versions of postmodernism and multiculturalism that preach the unavoidability of perspective, the inevitability of prejudice, and (therefore) the suspect status of any generally held view. (Postmodernism is liberalism taken seriously.) Whether or not conservative activists believe in this deconstruction of received authority (and by and large they don't), they are clever enough to appropriate it for their own purposes. If liberal polemicists can defend gay marriage by challenging the right of a church or a state to define what marriage is, why, the argument goes, can't Intelligent Design proponents demand equal time in the textbooks and the classroom by challenging the right of Ivy League professors or journal editors to say what science is?

Intelligent Designers are not the first denizens of the right to borrow arguments and strategies from the liberal and postmodern left. Holocaust deniers, to whom they are often compared (over 180,000 items on Google), were there before them. In the early '90s Holocaust denier Bradley Smith was able to place a series of ads (actually mini-essays) in college student newspapers in part because he presented his ideas under the heading "The Holocaust Controversy: The Case for Open Debate." Not the case for why there was no campaign to exterminate the Jews, not the case for why Hitler was innocent of any genocidal thoughts, not the case for why Holocaust-promoting Jews are just trying to drum up "financial support for Jewish causes" (all things asserted in the body of the ad), but the case for open debate, and how could anyone, and especially academics, be against that? Ours is not a "radical point of view," Smith asserts. We are just acting on premises that "were worked out some time ago during a little something called the Enlightenment." All we're saying, insists Mark Weber, another prominent denier, is, "Let's hear both sides." Don't "Americans have the right to judge the important issues for themselves?"

Proponents of Intelligent Design are rightly outraged when their efforts are linked to the efforts of Holocaust deniers, for there is no *moral* equivalence between the two projects. One, after all, is in the business of whitewashing genocide, while the other is in the business of giving to God the credit for having created the wonders of the physical world. (I know that Intelligent Design literature stays away from the word "God," but no one, in or out of the movement, thinks that the answer to the question "designed by whom?" is anything but God.) There is however an equivalence of strategy that makes the linking of the two inevitable: in both cases issues that have been settled in the relevant institutional precincts—departments of History and Biology, scientific journals, etc.—are reopened and finessed by reframing them as abstract philosophical questions: instead of "What is the evidence for the Holocaust having occurred and is it persuasive?" ask "Isn't debate something that should not be foreclosed?" Instead of "What data in the world of observation and experiment can be cited in support of Intelligent Design?" ask "Shouldn't explanatory accounts, even those disdained by mainstream researchers, be given equal time in our classrooms?" Intelligent Designers and Holocaust deniers, despite the differences between them, play the same shell game; they both say look *here*, in the highest reaches of speculation about inquiry in general, and not *there*, in the places where the particular, nitty-gritty work of empirical inquiry is actually being done. They both contrive to deflect criticism by moving immediately to a perspective so broad and all-inclusive that all claims are legitimized not because they have proven out in the competition of ideas but simply because someone is asserting them. When any claim has a right to be heard and taught just because it is one, judgment falls by the wayside and is replaced by the imperative to let a hundred (or a million) flowers bloom.

There's a word for this, and it's relativism. Polemicists on the right regularly lambaste left intellectuals for promoting relativism and its attendant bad practices—relaxing or abandoning standards, letting into the curriculum any idea no matter how outlandish so long as some constituency is attached to it, trashing received wisdom by impugning the motives of those who have established it, setting aside evidence that is inconvenient and putting in its place grand theories supported by nothing but the partisan beliefs and desires of the theorizers. Whether or not this is true of the right's targets, it is certainly true of the right itself, which turns relativist whenever its members invoke the mantras of "teach the controversies" or "keep the debate open" not out of a commitment to scrupulous scholarship (although that will be what is asserted) but in an effort to accomplish by misdirection and displacement what they could not accomplish by evidence and argument.

But didn't they learn it from the cultural left? And isn't the cultural left in part responsible for the flourishing of agendas it despises? This is certainly the view of historians like Deborah Lipstadt, who declares (in *Denying the Holocaust*) that the postmodern deconstruction of established authority "created an atmosphere of permissiveness toward the questioning of historical events and made it hard . . . to assert that there is anything 'off limits' for this skeptical approach." Science writer Joe Kaplinsky makes the same point when he observes that when creationists (by whatever name) call into question the motives of mainstream researchers, they have been taught to do so by left radicals "who pioneered the idea that . . . claims to expertise generally were little more than an excuse to assert power by marginalizing the voice of the victim." In short, once the corrosive skepticism of postmodern thought is let loose, nothing is safe from its leveling force.

Yes and no. Yes, it is the case that postmodern thought (as the logical extension of liberal thought) delegitimates the claim of any account to be exhaustive, complete, and invulnerable to challenge. The reasoning (a version of fallibilism) is that because accounts emerge in the course of history and come to us in vocabularies that belong to a particular moment in the adventure of inquiry, it is always possible, and perhaps even probable, that in time new vocabularies will replace the old ones and bring with them new, and newly authoritative, accounts.

So far so good. The mistake, and it is one made by some postmodern thinkers and seized upon by their neoconservative opponents, is to go from this perfectly ordinary description of how knowledge is established, tested, and sometimes dislodged—this, after all, *is* the scientific method—to the extraordinary and unearned conclusion that nothing that has been established as knowledge is to be trusted. The essence of the mistake is to think that the inevitable and blameless historicity of all accounts relativizes them with respect to measures like accuracy, trustworthiness, validity, and legitimacy. But postmodern thought places all accounts on an equal footing only in the sense that it renders them equally historical—equally the products of human judgment—which means that none of them is the result of a direct, unmediated encounter with reality as it exists apart from any human, temporally bounded vocabulary whatsoever. That said, however, all the important differences remain, the differences that arise from the different projects of inquiry in relation to which the different vocabularies have been developed. Sociology, political science, anthropology, literary criticism, the law, science, theology—all these areas of investigation have their own particular histories that include procedures and tests for assessing the worth and value of proposed contributions to the enterprise. These procedures and tests are typically specific to the project to whose urgencies they are a response. Literary critics want to find out what a poem means. Political scientists want to find out what motivates voters. Lawyers and legal theorists worry about how to determine whether or not a proposed statute is constitutional. Scientists hazard and test hypotheses in an effort to lay bare the structures of the material world. There is of course some commerce between these enterprises—they are not hermetically sealed islands—but the decorums and accepted routines of one cannot easily be transferred to another.

A doctrinaire postmodernist might respond by saying that the lines between disciplines have themselves been drawn in history by fallible men and women. They are a product of human judgment and therefore can always be redrawn. Yes, but you don't redraw a line simply by saying that it is possible to redraw it. The actual work of marshaling evidence and making arguments in support of a newly drawn line must still be done, and postmodernism has nothing to contribute to that work. Postmodernism is a general and abstract description of the way knowledge is established and challenged. It tells us that any establishing or challenging of knowledge is a historical rather than a transcendent event. But postmodernism is not itself decisive in either effort. It is neither a challenge to nor an affirmation of any conclusion historically situated agents have reached because it itself has no historical content. That is, one cannot rehearse the tenets of postmodernism and then adduce a "therefore" that is directed at some matter of fact. Nothing you might say in response to questions like "what is your theory of truth?" or "is there a reality independent of cultural perspectives?" will have the slightest influence on how you proceed when you are asked to produce an interpretation of a poem, or write an account of an historical event, or replicate the results of a laboratory experiment. You can be persuaded by postmodern arguments on the very general level of their usual assertion—everything is mediated, everything comes to us under a description, the stipulation of fact is always perspective-specific—and you can still hold firmly to judgments of truth, accuracy, correctness, and error as they are made in the precincts of some particular realm of inquiry.

Both the left and the right (for different reasons) have a stake in believing that postmodern thought has consequences, either good or bad. The left wants to believe that postmodernism undermines or calls into question all settled structures of knowledge and authority. The right takes left-postmodernists at their word because it wants to believe that those who rehearse postmodern arguments are the sworn enemies of the good and the true. But postmodern thought is without consequences for anything. It troubles no present arrangement of things. It is not the answer to any locally posed question. It will not direct you to strike out in either this or that direction as you begin your investigation. It will not authorize or stand in the way of any agenda. Outside the rarified precincts in which it competes with other high-level philosophical theses, postmodern thought does no real work at all. It does, however, do rhetorical and political work. That is, it can be employed either as a resource, or as an accusation, or as a diversion by someone who is looking to score points.

That is why postmodernism and deconstruction are so often invoked as "scare words" by neoconservative polemicists who believe that by attacking them, they are attacking an agenda embraced by the intellectual left. But neither postmodernism nor deconstruction is an agenda; they are epistemological arguments.

The argument, basically, is that the structures of intelligibility in which we more or less unselfconsciously live—the coherences that seem to present themselves naturally to us as we look at and move about in the world—are not natural at all, are not the result of the world's pre-existing patterns of meaning imprinting themselves on our perception, but are constructed. They are not constructed by anyone in particular (this is not a conspiracy theory), but by traditions of inquiry, practice, and rhetoric that in time acquire enough traction and perdurability to become components in our storehouse of common sense. Once this state has been achieved (again by no one in particular), an idea or a behavior or an agenda that might have earlier been seen as new or odd or even bizarre becomes part of the landscape, becomes naturalized, becomes what we think *within* rather than what we think *about*, and it takes a special effort (which in the ordinary course of things few will make) to return us to the moment when something now in the category of "the taken for granted" or "what goes without saying" was seen as strange, unassimilated, and a candidate for possible rejection. That special effort is sometimes called simply "critique" and sometimes called "deconstruction" (although it was certainly available to human beings long before deconstruction was a concept), a word that has nothing to do with destruction (a mistake commonly made), but with the activity of showing how a part of our experience that seems given and inevitable was, in fact, constructed by human agents. Deconstruction undoes, at least analytically, that act of construction and lays bare (or at least that is the claim) its origins in history. (I should add that this is only one strain of deconstructionist thought.)

An example might help, and I turn to what might seem an unlikely source, the comedian Bob Newhart. When he came up in the '50s, Newhart was a standup comic whose prop was a telephone. He would appear on stage with the telephone and take a phone call from some historical personage with whom he would then engage in conversation; you knew what his interlocutor was saying because Newhart would repeat it, often in a tone of incredulity, before responding. In one of his more famous routines he is a functionary in the government of Queen Elizabeth I talking to Sir Walter Raleigh, who has for some time been in the New World conducting an expedition funded by the Crown. What he wants to find out is whether the government is getting anything for its money. Accordingly, he asks Raleigh if he has discovered the passage to India or at least some gold, and when the answer is "no" to both, he explodes in exasperation, "Don't you have *anything* for us, Walter?" Raleigh's reply is delivered in piecemeal to the audience as Newhart's character finds himself unable to believe any of it. "What's that, Walter, you've discovered a leaf? It grows in the ground? You pick it, you roll it up, and—am I hearing this right, Walter?—you put it in your mouth and LIGHT IT ON FIRE!!?"

What Newhart is doing, obviously, is zeroing in on a practice—the smoking of cigarettes—that was in the 1950s when he performed the routine so familiar a part of the American landscape that no one (except for a few medical researchers) ever thought much about it or contested its right to exist; and by means of his theatricalized (and anachronistic) telephone conversation, he is taking us back imaginatively to the world as it was before that practice became so habitual as to be nearly invisible. He is, in short, deconstructing it, showing that it is not natural, did not come with the moon and the stars, and, in a formulation dear to early practitioners of deconstruction, could have been otherwise, indeed, could have not been at all.

The example allows me to make several points. First, this act of deconstruction was performed before anyone had uttered the word deconstruction (although the early twentieth-century Russian Formalists employed a similar technique they called "defamiliarization," probably a better term), which tells us that whatever it is, deconstruction is not an arcane academic practice, but a practice engaged in by anyone who for some reason is struck by the oddity of a piece of behavior accepted uncritically by society.

My second point is that Newhart's routine would not be effective today, in the twenty-first century, because the practice that is its object no longer has the naturalized status it once enjoyed. You might say that smoking has been deconstructed in the past thirty years by the very culture of which it was once an integral and barely remarked part. (Remember everyone in *Casablanca, The Maltese Falcon, Gentlemen's Agreement,* and *The Best Years of Our Lives* puffing away merrily?) It is sometimes charged (by Lipstadt, for example) that deconstruction is the enemy of history and of historical fact (and thereby guilty of undermining the academic endeavor). But the reverse is true: deconstruction is an investigation into the way facts have been historically produced, the way they have passed from the state of hypotheses or strange new assertions to the stage of being so ordinary and undoubted and here-to-stay that no one thinks to pay them any particular attention, and the conditions that might lead to their regaining the status of the anomalous and the deviant.

My third point is that deconstruction or critique is not politically inflected. As a technique for uncovering occluded and forgotten assumptions, it is available both to the left and to the right. To be sure, this is not its public face; for in the public mind, deconstruction is associated with the left and with radical nihilism. This was the case in spades in the days following September 11, 2001. Who would have thought in those first few minutes, hours, days that what we now call 9/11 was to become an event in the culture wars? Now years later, nothing could be clearer, though it was only on September 22, 2001, that the first sign appeared, in a *New York Times* opinion piece written by Edward Rothstein and entitled "Attacks on U.S. Challenge the Perspectives of Postmodern True Believers." A few days later (on September 27), Julia Keller wrote a smaller piece in the *Chicago Tribune*; her title: "After the Attack, Postmodernism Loses Its Glib Grip." In the September 24 issue of *Time*, Roger Rosenblatt announced "the end of the age of irony" and predicted that "the good folks in charge of America's intellectual life" would now have to change their tune and no longer say that "nothing was real" or that "nothing was to be believed in or taken seriously." And on October 1, John Leo, in a piece entitled "Campus Hand-Wringing Is Not a Pretty Sight," blamed just about everything on the "very dangerous ideas" that have captured our "campus culture"; to wit, "radical cultural relativism, nonjudgmentalism, and a postmodern conviction that there are no moral norms or truths worth defending."

Well, that certainly sounds bad—no truths, no knowledge, no reality, no morality, no judgments, no objectivity—and if postmodernists are saying that, they are not so much dangerous as silly. Postmodernists, however, say no such thing, and what they do say, if it is understood at all, is unlikely to provoke either the anger or the alarm of our modern Paul Reveres. Most of the time, it is not understood. Rothstein tells us (without benefit of any citations) that "postmodernists challenge assertions that truth and ethical judgment have any objective validity." Well, it depends on what you mean by "objective." If you mean a standard of validity and value that is independent of any historically emergent and therefore revisable system of thought and practice, then it is true that many postmodernists would deny that any such standard is or could ever be available. But if by "objective" one means a standard of validity and value that is backed up by the tried-and-true procedures and protocols of a well-developed practice or discipline—history, physics, economics, psychology, etc.—then such standards are all around us, and we make use of them all the time without any metaphysical anxiety.

As Richard Rorty, one of Rothstein's targets, was fond of saying, "Objectivity is the kind of thing we do around here." That is, objectivity is just another name for trying to get something right in a particular area of inquiry. Historians draw conclusions about the meaning of events, astronomers present models of planetary movements, psychologists offer accounts of the reading process, consumers make decisions about which product is best, parents choose schools for their children—all of these things and many more are done with varying degrees of confidence, and in no case is the confidence rooted in a philosophical account (positive or skeptical) of objectivity. Rather, the researcher begins in some context of practice, with its received authorities, sacred texts, exemplary achievements, and generally accepted benchmarks, and from within the perspective (and not within the perspective of a general theory) of that context—thick, interpersonal, densely elaborated—judges something to be true or inaccurate, reasonable or irrational, and so on.

It seems, then, that the unavailability of an absolutely objective vantage point, of a god's eye view, doesn't take anything away from us. If, as postmodernists sometimes assert, objective standards of a publicly verifiable kind are unavailable, they are so only in the sense that they have always been unavailable (this is not, in other words, a condition postmodernism has caused), and we have always managed to get along without them, doing a great many things despite the fact that we might be unable to shore them up in accordance with the most rigorous philosophical demands.

Now, I would not be misunderstood. I am not saying that there are no universal values or no truths independent of particular perspectives. I am saying that whatever universal values and independent truths there may be (and I believe in both), they are not acknowledged by everyone and no mechanism exists that would result in their universal acceptance. When I offer a reading of a poem or pronounce on a case in First Amendment law, I do so with no epistemological reservations. I regard my reading as true—not provisionally true, or true for my reference group only, but true. But I am just as certain that I may very well be unable to persuade others, no less educated or credentialed than I, of the truth so perspicuous to me. And here is a point that is often missed, the independence from each other of two assertions thought to be contradictory: (1) I believe X to be true and (2) I believe that there is no mechanism, procedure, calculus, test, by which the truth of X can be necessarily demonstrated to any sane person who has come to a different conclusion (not that such a demonstration can never be successful, only that its success is contingent and not necessary). In order to assert something and mean it without qualification, I of course have to believe that it is true, but I don't have to believe that I could demonstrate its truth to all rational persons. (Persuasion is a contingent matter.) The claim that something is universal and the acknowledgment that I couldn't necessarily prove it are logically independent of each other. The second does not undermine the first.

Once again, then, a postmodern argument turns out to be without any deleterious consequences (it is also without any positive consequences), and it certainly does not stand in the way of condemning those who have proven themselves to be our enemies in words and deeds. Nor should this be surprising, for, after all, as I have noted, postmodernism is a series of arguments, not a way of life or a recipe for action. Your belief or disbelief in postmodern tenets is independent of your beliefs and commitments in any other area of your life. You may believe that objectivity of an absolute kind is possible or you may believe that it is not, but when you have to decide whether a particular thing is true or false, neither belief will hinder or help you. What will help you are archives, exemplary achievements, revered authorities, official bodies of evidence, relevant analogies, suggestive metaphors—all available to all persons independently of their philosophical convictions, or of the fact that they do or do not have any.

If postmodernism does not have the metaphysical consequences claimed for it by its detractors, neither can it have the consequence of promoting unpatriotic behavior, an accusation made by William Bennett, former secretary of education, in his book *Why We Fight: Moral Clarity and the War on Terrorism* (2002). In this book we learn that the problems not only of the current moment but of the last forty years stem from the cultural ascendancy of those "who are unpatriotic" but who, unfortunately, are also "the most influential among us." The phrase "among us" is a nice illustration of the double game Bennett plays throughout the book. On one reading, "the diversity mongers [and] multi-culturalists," mistaken though they may be in their views, are part of "us"; that is, they are citizens, participating with the rest of us in the back and forth of deliberative democracy. On another reading, however, these cultural relativists are "among us" as a fifth column might be among us, servants of an alien power who prosecute their subversive agenda under the false colors of citizenship. That the second is the reading Bennett finally intends (though he wants to get moral credit for the first) is made clear when he charges these peddlers of "relativism" with unpatriotism, and in that instant defines a patriot as someone who has the same views he has.

This also turns out to be Bennett's definition of honesty and truth-telling. As the remedy for what he and his allies see as the moral enervation of the country, Bennett urges "the reinstatement of a thorough and honest study of our history," where by "honest" he means a study of history that tells the same story he and his friends would tell if they were in control of the nation's history departments. Unfortunately (at least as he sees it), history departments are full of people like Columbia's Eric Foner, who drew Bennett's ire for wondering which is worse, "the horror that engulfed New York City or the apocalyptic rhetoric emanating daily from the White House." Bennett calls this sentiment "atrocious rot." Maybe it is, maybe it isn't, but even if it were atrocious rot, it could be honest atrocious rot; that is, it could be Foner's honest attempt, as a citizen and historian, to take the truthful measure of what the events of September 11 and their aftermath mean. But in Bennett's view, Foner and all the other "Foners of the United States" are not merely mistaken (which is how we usually characterize those on the opposite side of us in what John Milton called the "wars of truth"); they are "insidious," they are engaged in "violent misrepresentation," they practice "distortion," they "sow widespread and debilitating confusion," they "weaken the country's resolve," they exhibit "failures of character," they drown out "legitimate patriots," they display a "despicable nature," they abandon "the honest search for truth."

This long list of hit-and-run accusations is directed at those who would give different answers than Bennett would to questions still being honestly debated seven years later. It is one thing to believe that someone has gotten something wrong; it is quite another to believe that the someone you think to be wrong is by virtue of that error unpatriotic, devoted to lies, and downright evil.

There is a tension in Bennett's book—one common to jeremiads on the right—between his frequent assertions that our cultural condition couldn't be worse and his equally frequent assertions that the vast majority of Americans thinks as he does. How can the enemy at once be so small in number and so disastrously effective? The answer is to be found in the fact that this small band controls our colleges and universities, and the result is the "utter failure of our institutions of higher learning," a failure the product of which is a generation of college students ignorant of our history and imbued with the virus of "cultural and moral relativism." In the pages of the *Wall Street Journal*, the *Washington Times*, the *American Enterprise*, and other venues, alarms are sounded because, according to surveys, 85 percent to 97 percent of faculty members in the humanities and social sciences departments of our most prestigious universities identify themselves as left of center.

If these figures are correct (and I believe they are), they raise at least three questions: How has this happened? What does it mean for hiring and instruction in our universities? And what, if anything, should be done about it?

To the first question, those who report the survey results and proclaim "the shame of America's one-party campuses" have a simple answer: it's a vast left-wing conspiracy, part of "a gigantic social machine working to push society to the left," according to Robert Locke of FrontPageMagazine.com.

To the second question, Locke and his colleagues give essentially the same answer: colleges and universities conspire by offering "academic employment to liberals only." But if you know how the hiring process works, this accusation makes no sense. Departments are required by law to advertise a position and consider all applications. Applicants are asked to provide transcripts, writing samples, and recommendations from senior scholars.

On the basis of these materials, a search committee selects three or four finalists who are brought to campus and questioned closely about their teaching and research interests. No inquiry into an applicant's political allegiances is made or allowed. As a dean, I interviewed more than three hundred job seekers, and although I found out a lot about their research and teaching agendas, I couldn't have told you anything about their political agendas if my life depended on it.

It's not just that universities don't set out to hire only liberals; it's that they couldn't implement that resolve even if they had it. You can't apply a political test if you know nothing about the politics of those in your pool.

But so what? someone might reply. No matter how they got there, liberals are in the classroom, where, laments Walter Williams in the *Washington Times*, they now teach America's sons and daughters "that the Founders of the United States were fascists," that literature "written by 'dead white men' is a tool of exploitation," and that "one person's vision of reality is just as valid as another's."

But this inference from politics to pedagogy holds only if it is assumed that once you know how someone voted in the last election you also will know what and how they teach. And that assumption does not hold. The fact that someone voted Democratic or Republican in an election will tell you nothing about his or her position on the questions that are an academic's stock in trade, questions such as: Is the ability to use language hard-wired? Was the Civil War an economic struggle? Do voters respond negatively to negative advertising? Someone on either side of these or a thousand other questions could have voted Republican, or Democratic, or Libertarian, or Green, or may not have voted at all. There is no necessary or even likely correlation between the political views of a faculty member and the views he or she may have on a disputed issue in an academic field.

In 2000 I was a registered Democrat and voted for Gore. In 2000 I also completed a book portraying the English poet John Milton as a conservative, hard-core Christian authoritarian. I am not a conservative hard-core Christian, but I believe Milton was one, and it is the truth about Milton that I'm trying to get at when I write and teach. My understanding of what that truth is has nothing whatsoever to do with the way I voted, and I could change my mind about Milton and still remain a Democrat or I could become a Republican and have exactly the views about Milton I have now. Of course there always will be some faculty members who are political liberals and who also have been persuaded by postmodern arguments, but this coincidence of political and intellectual commitments is just that—coincidental—and by no means certain.

So the twin bases of the neoconservative complaint collapse: the fact of a predominantly liberal faculty says nothing necessarily about what the faculty teaches, and the faculty is not the product of some giant leftist social machine. But the question remains, what is it the product of?

The answer is a history too complicated to tell here, but it would include the GI Bill of Rights, which gave people like me—children of working-class immigrants—the opportunity to attend college and enter the professorate, bringing with them the largely union politics they grew up in. It also would include the waves of feminist, black, Hispanic, and gay activism that brought hitherto underrepresented and therefore politically active ethnic populations into the academy. The '60s "radicals" who transferred the idealism of their political hopes to the idealism of a transformative theory of education make up another element of the answer.

These were not planned events and patterns; they just occurred, and when the dust settled, the academy—or at least the liberal arts side of it—had become the home of many people who thought of themselves as progressive and on the left.

This brings us finally to the third question: what should be done about it?

Since "it" is not the result of Machiavellian design and does not entail the dire consequences feared by our modern Cassandras and Chicken Littles, there doesn't seem to be a real need to do anything. And we certainly should not do what the neoconservatives urge us to do—insist on "an approximate equality in the numbers of left-of-center and right-of-center faculty" (Robert Locke).

Ideological or political balance, I say once again, is not a legitimate goal for an academic institution any more than it would be for a corporate boardroom (where, I suspect, the relevant statistics would be more cheering to the conservative heart), and in both cases the reason is the same: that's not the business they're in.

Corporations are in the business of expanding markets and turning profits. Universities are in the business of producing and disseminating knowledge. The issue for both will not be what your politics are, but whether you know what you're doing and are doing it well.

Still, it might be argued that even if the liberal faculty is an accident of history and that faculty's teaching does not exist in a causal relationship with its politics, it would be a good thing if there were more conservatives in the mix. That might be a reasonable social goal, but the trick would be to achieve it. Because it cannot legitimately be the goal of a university to enforce a political balance in its faculty, the strategies employed must come from the supply side.

I can think of two.

The Heritage Foundation, the American Enterprise Institute, or other well-funded, highly organized outfits on the right might send waves of recruiters to the nation's high schools, where they would seek out bright, ambitious young conservatives and urge them to consider a career teaching French poetry or the economics of the Weimar Republic.

The second strategy is more likely to work and is one I heartily endorse: the same organizations could lobby for an increase in academic entry salaries from the current $50,000 to $60,000 range to something in the range of $150,000 to infinity.

Add to that a few perks like condos in Aspen, company yachts, junkets to Tahiti, and personal research budgets in the high six figures and put it all into a package with the academic equivalent of stock options, and I'll bet that in a very short time the political profile of the professorate will look satisfyingly different to those who now complain about a faculty that tilts to the left.

I doubt that those on the right will take up my suggestions, if only because complaining is what they like to do, and in 2007, they were doing it in a film called *Indoctrinate U*, directed by Evan Coyne Maloney. You may think that universities are places where ideas are explored and evaluated in a spirit of objective inquiry. But in fact, Maloney tells us, they are places of indoctrination where a left-leaning faculty teaches every subject, including chemistry and horticulture, through the prism of race, class, and gender; where minorities and women are taught that they are victims of oppression; where admissions policies are racially gerrymandered; where identity-based programs reproduce the patterns of segregation that the left supposedly abhors; where students and faculty who speak against the prevailing orthodoxy are ostracized, disciplined, and subjected to sensitivity training; where conservative speakers like Ward Connerly are shouted down; where radical speakers like Ward Churchill are welcomed; where speech codes mandate speech that offends no one; where the faculty preaches diversity but is itself starkly homogeneous with respect to political affiliation; where professors regularly use the classroom as a platform for their political views; where students parrot back the views they know their instructors to hold; where course reading lists are heavy on radical texts and light on texts celebrating the Western tradition; where the American flag is held in suspicion; where military recruiting personnel are either treated rudely or barred from campus; where the default assumption is that anything the United States and Israel do is evil.

This is a large bill of particulars, but hardly a new one; Alan Bloom, Dinesh D'Souza, Roger Kimball, Charles Sykes, Lynne Cheney, Alan Kors, Anne Neal, and David Horowitz, among others, precede Maloney—and while each of the complaints is presented as equally weighty, some are more significant than others and a few are red herrings.

The question of who gets to speak on campus is one of them. Speakers are typically invited to campus by departments and by elected student committees charged with the responsibility of distributing student fees. One group decides what work in the discipline is important and cutting-edge; the other decides more on the basis of popularity and notoriety. Neither is particularly interested in balance; nor should they be.

Balance requires that you ask the question, "Did every con-stituency get its turn or its share?" But to ask that question is to replace judgment with the criterion of proportional represen-tation, and in the academy that is almost always a bad idea.

As for the clannishness of students who hang out only with those of their own race and ethnicity, that is certainly wor-risome, and it is likely that the strong marking of identity in admissions policies, course descriptions, and race- or gender-based centers contributes to it. But to call it segregation is to fudge the distinction between forced separation and a separa-tion voluntarily chosen (even if it is a separation you lament). Maloney does exactly this when he reports on racially skewed admissions practices while his screen shows grainy-imaged footage of the pre–*Brown v. Board of Education* days. They're the same, he's saying. No they're not.

Then there's the matter of speech codes. This is a fake issue. Every speech code that has been tested in the courts has been struck down, often on the very grounds—you can't criminalize offensiveness—invoked by Maloney. Even though there are such codes on the books of some universi-ties, attempts to enforce them will never hold up. Students don't have to worry about speech codes. The universities that have them do, a point made by *Indoctrinate U* when Maloney tells the story of how Cal Poly was taken to the cleaners when it tried to discipline a student for putting up a poster with the word "plantation" in it.

Another red herring is the accusation that there is too little patriotism on campus. Maloney interviews a bus driver who was forced by a university to remove an American flag because it might make foreign students uncomfortable. Removing a flag from a university bus may be an act the wisdom of which might be questioned, but the question would go to the university's competence, not its patrio-tism. (There is a difference between being stupid and being disloyal.) Universities by definition are neither patriotic nor unpatriotic; striking political stances in either direction is not the business they are properly in.

Still, when all the red herrings and nonissues have been checked off, there remain some serious questions. Why, Maloney asks, should "schools pay people to operate offices and programs that are blatantly political in nature?" (He has in mind offices and programs like Women's Studies, Gay and Lesbian Studies, African American Studies, Chicano Studies.)

The answer to that question is to pose two others: (1) Are there in fact programs with those names that are more political than academic? (2) Do programs with those names have to be more political than academic?

The answer to the first question is yes, to the second no. It is certainly the case that many of these programs gained a place in the academy through political activism, but that doesn't mean that once they are in place political activism need be, or should be, the content of their activities. Race, gender, and class are serious topics and as such worthy of serious study. There are more than enough legitimate academic projects to keep an ethnic or gender studies department going for decades—the recovery of lost texts, the history of economic struggle and success, the relationship of race, ethnicity, and gender to medical research. And there is no reason in principle that such investigations must begin or end in accusations against capitalism, the white male Protestant establishment, and the U.S. government.

But some of them do. Some of these programs forget what the prupose of a university is and continue to think of themselves as extensions of a political agenda. And students who take courses in those programs may well feel the pressure of that agenda. When that happens, an administration should step in and stop it. And if it doesn't, it deserves every criticism this documentary levels.

How many such programs are there? Maloney strongly implies that they are all like that but offers little evidence except the anecdotal evidence of the dozen or so people he interviews. In other places in his documentary he offers as evidence the familiar (and, as I have acknowledged, accurate) statistics indicating that in many departments 75 percent to 95 percent of the faculty self-identifies as left of center. Noting that Stanford's Diversity Office advertises itself as promoting difference, Maloney guesses that "it isn't doing such a great job," given that in the humanities Democrats outnumber Republicans 144 to 10. He quotes a student who declares, "The university totally ignores that diversity of thought means political diversity."

No it doesn't. Political diversity means that in terms of its partisan affiliations, a university faculty should look like America and display the same balance of Democrats and Republicans as can be found in the country's voting rolls. But this requirement of proportional political representation makes sense only if ballot box performance predicts and tracks classroom performance. And, as I have already pointed out, it does not. In many social science departments, there is a split right down the middle between partisans of quantitative methods (techniques like statistical modeling) and partisans of qualitative methods (inquiries rooted in philosophy and theory). But, as the statistics Maloney cites show, 90 percent of those on either side of this divide will be registered Democrats. What this means is that knowing the political registration of a faculty member tells you nothing necessarily about the way in which he or she teaches. (Academic commitments and partisan commitments are independent variables.)

Still, "necessarily" is an important qualifier, and as *Indoctrinate U* makes clear, there are those who do not distinguish between academic and partisan politics and allow the latter to inflect the former, often in the name of social justice. Once again, the question is how many of them are there? Anne Neal, president of the conservative watch-dog group the American Council of Trustees and Alumni, asks that question on camera and answers it by reporting that in a survey of students a "significant percentage...complained that politics was being introduced in the classroom" and 42 percent "said their book lists were one-sided."

Here, again, we have the part that should be taken seriously and the red-herring or fake-issue part. Book lists take their shape from the instructor's judgment that a particular text is important to the area of inquiry. There is no reason—at least no pedagogical reason—to demand that a book list contain representatives of every approach out there. But we should take seriously the part about professors who use the classroom as a stage for their political views. Maloney speculates that perhaps one out of seven performs in this way. I would put the number much lower, perhaps one out of twenty-five. But one out of ten thousand would be one too many.

Academics often bridle at the picture of their activities presented by Maloney, and other conservative critics and accuse them of grossly caricaturing and exaggerating what goes on in the classroom. Maybe so, but so long as there are those who confuse advocacy with teaching, and so long as faculty colleagues and university administrators look the other way, the academy invites the criticism it receives in this documentary. In 1915, the American Association of University Professors warned that if we didn't clean up our own shop, external constituencies, with motives more political than educational, would step in and do it for us. Now they're doing it in the movies and it's our own fault.

# SIX

# Higher Education under Attack

So I return in the end to my one-note song: if academics did only the job they are trained and paid to do—introduce students to disciplinary materials and equip them with the necessary analytic skills—criticism of the kind Maloney mounts would have no object, and the various watch-dog groups headed by David Horowitz, Daniel Pipes, and others would have to close shop. But even if this day were to arrive, the academy would not be home free because there would still be the problem I have alluded to but not fully addressed—the problem of money. Who is going to pay for the purified academic enterprise I celebrate in these pages? The unhappy fact is that the more my fellow academics obey the imperative always to academicize, the less they will have a claim to a skeptical public's support.

How do you sell to legislators, governors, trustees, donors, newspapers, etc., an academy that marches to its own drummer, an academy that asks of the subjects that petition for entry only that they be interesting, an academy unconcerned with the public yield of its activities, an academy that puts at the center of its operations the asking of questions for their own sake? How, that is, do you justify the enterprise? As I have already pointed out, you can't, in part because the demand for justification never comes from the inside. The person who asks you to justify what you do is not saying, "tell me why *you* value the activity," but "convince me that *I* should," and if you respond in the spirit of that request, you will have exchanged your values for those of your inquisitor. It may seem paradoxical to say so, but any justification of the academy is always a denigration of it. The only honest thing to do when someone from the outside asks, "what use is this venture anyway?" is to answer "none whatsoever," if by "use" is meant (as it always will be) of use to those with no investment in the obsessions internal to the profession. That answer will surely sound strangely in the ears of donors and those who remember that many public universities were established (by the Morrill and Hatch Acts) with a declared expectation of what they would do for the state. Nevertheless, it is the only answer that respects and preserves the academy's autonomy.

This is not the answer that will by itself reverse the trend of the past forty years, which have seen revenues systematically withdrawn from public education. In January of 2002, Mark Yudof, then president of the University of Minnesota, wrote an essay for the *Chronicle of Higher Education* titled, "Is the Public Research University Dead?" Now, six years later, the most optimistic answer one could give is "Not yet."

The key word in Yudof's title is "public," which has traditionally been short for "state supported." There's both the rub and the question: in an era of declining state support, when is it no longer accurate to designate an institution "public"?

George M. Dennison, president of the University of Montana at Missoula, recalls that in the '60s and '70s the usual assumption was "that the public should pay from 70 percent to 80 percent of the cost of higher education." Now the figure is more likely to be 25 percent (if you're lucky), and in some states the figure is 10 and headed downward. Only ten years ago, Dennison reports, the ratio of state-appropriated funds to tuition dollars in his state was 3 to 1. Now it is 2 to 1 in the other direction: "$1 of state appropriations for every $2 of tuition and fees."

The university's expenditures, Dennison says, have increased markedly, in part because of a large increase in the number of students it is asked to serve; but "fully 98 percent of the increased funding has come from tuition and fees and private support, not from the state."

The story is the same everywhere, despite what some irresponsible politicians sometimes say. Even in those states where the raw sums expended on higher education have been rising, the percentage of the budget devoted to higher education—the figure that means something because it reflects general changes in the cost of doing business and providing services—is declining.

In Wisconsin and other states the level of state support has been more than halved in the past fifteen years. The dilemma was summed up by Katharine C. Lyall, retired chancellor of the University of Wisconsin system: "They want high access, low tuition, top quality, and no tax increases to pay for it."

The result, as Yudof puts it, is a breaking of the compact negotiated long ago by state governments and public research universities: "In return for financial support from taxpayers, universities agreed to keep tuition low and provide access for students from a broad range of economic backgrounds, train graduate and professional students, promote arts and culture, help solve problems in the community, and perform groundbreaking research."

That's a tall order and, up to now, the universities have pretty much been doing their part—giving educational opportunities to millions who would have otherwise been denied them—but in recent years they have been largely abandoned by their partners. Nevertheless, universities are regularly told to make do with what they have, tighten their belts, become more efficient, eliminate frills, teach more, and pay less.

The result is predictable, and you can read about it in your daily newspaper: the very legislators who have withdrawn the money now turn around and berate universities for not providing what they are unwilling to pay for. "It's outrageous," said Richard S. Jarvis, then chancellor of the Oregon University System, "that the state should become a minority partner in educating its undergraduates."

In 2003, Republican representatives John A. Boehner (later to become majority leader of his party) and Howard McKeon issued a report that, if taken seriously, would have the effect of accelerating the decline Jarvis laments. The spirit presiding over this report is not the spirit of academic autonomy, but the spirit of consumer capitalism. Entitled the "College Cost Crisis," the report asserts that higher education costs are "skyrocketing" and the reason is "wasteful spending" by colleges and universities.

It is certainly true that college costs are rising. The first question is, are the increases disproportionate to increases in other sectors—housing, transportation, food, travel, entertainment, books, medical care, prescription drugs? (The answer is "No.") And second, do colleges and universities charge more because they have to pay more for the goods and services necessary to their operation? Had they bothered to ask, McKeon and Boehner would have found that the answer to the second question is a very big "Yes."

Utility costs are way up, insurance costs (especially for university medical centers) have more than doubled, and the tab for constructing new buildings and renovating or maintaining old ones is out of sight. New security costs have been mandated (but not funded) in the wake of September 11. The cost of information systems—barely on the horizon in the '70s, the report's favored decade and a time when student registration was still being done manually in the gym— is now astronomical. The cost of materials and equipment, especially for the new technologies that come with the new sciences (nano technology, neuroscience, bio-everything) developed in the past three decades is soaring. And of course the cost of putting faculty members in the classrooms is higher than it used to be, especially in the increasing number of areas (like computer science, finance, management, engineering) where higher education has to compete for personnel with the corporate sector.

Not only have the costs of these materials and services escalated, but universities are forced to buy more of them because the number of students they are asked to accommodate has grown and continues to grow. Because Boehner and McKeon take no account at all of any of these changes in the real costs of doing business—changes the universities did not impose, but changes they must live with—the statistics they invoke with such a flourish are meaningless, or, rather, they are meaningful only within the bizarre and ignorant assumption that everything in the world of higher education is the same as it was in 1970 except for the price of the entry ticket.

If the methodology of the report is shoddy, the assumptions that drive it are even worse. One assumption is that colleges and universities should be responsive to what Americans believe, as in "Americans believe wasteful spending by college and university management is the No. 1 reason for skyrocketing college costs." But if what Americans believe is false (as it is in this instance), colleges and universities, rather than taking that falsehood seriously and conforming their actions to it, should labor to remove it; they should engage in education, not pandering.

To be sure, the study of what Americans believe is something that advertisers, vendors, and politicians are right to be interested in, and it can even be a proper academic subject, but it should not be what drives the academy's actions. It is entirely appropriate for General Motors, despite the number of people who (like me) are fans of Oldsmobile, to cease producing that automobile because its public image—what Americans believe about it—translates into poor sales. It is not appropriate for a university, an academic not a mercantile enterprise, to decide that because classics, history, German, French, American literature, anthropology, political science, and philosophy (among others) are little valued by many Americans and bring in little, if any, revenues, they should be eliminated.

Yet that is exactly what would happen (and in some places is already happening) if the second large assumption informing the Boehner-McKeon report—the assumption that colleges and universities should run their shops as if they were businesses—were taken to heart.

This too, according to the report, is something Americans believe: "Americans believe institutions of higher learning are not accountable enough to parents, students, and taxpayers—the consumers of higher education." But parents, students, and taxpayers are consumers of higher education only in the sense that they pay for it if they want it; they are not consumers in the sense that the operations of higher education should reflect either their desires or their judgments.

When I go to buy a new suit I know in advance what I want and need—something for work, something for leisure, something for a wedding—and I visit various vendors in order to compare products and prices. By definition, however, the recipients of higher education do not know in advance what they need. If they did, they wouldn't need it, and what they often want, at least at the outset, is an education that will tax their energies as little as possible.

Should educators give it to them? Absolutely not. Should curricular matters—questions of what subjects should be studied, what courses should be required, how large classes should be—be settled by surveying student preferences or polling their parents or asking Representatives Boehner and McKeon? No, again.

If colleges and universities are to be "accountable" to anyone or anything, it should be to the academic values— dedicated and responsible teaching, rigorous and honest research—without which higher education would be little different from the bottom-line enterprise its critics would have it become.

By the evidence of this report—not the evidence in the report; there's precious little of that—Boehner and McKeon wouldn't recognize an academic value if it ran over them. Indeed the word "academic" scarcely appears in what they write (if they wrote it), and perhaps this is how it should be, given a performance as slipshod and superficial as theirs is.

"Slipshod" and "superficial" are words not strong enough to describe the Web site the legislators set up as a "resource" addendum to their report. The centerpiece of the Web site—College Cost Central: A Resource for Parents, Students, & Taxpayers Fed Up with the High Costs of Higher Education—is a list of twelve yes/no questions to which those same parents, students, and taxpayers are asked to respond. Only three of the questions are real. The others are designed to elicit—no coerce—responses that can then be used to support the conclusions McKeon and Boehner have reached in advance of doing any research at all. Here, for example, is question 1: "Can colleges and universities be doing more to control their spending and avoid large tuition hikes that hurt parents and students?" Although this has the form of a question, its core content is four unsubstantiated assertions: (1) colleges and universities do not control their spending; (2) uncontrolled spending is the sole cause of tuition hikes; (3) those hikes are large (in relation to what norms or practices is never specified); and (4) they hurt parents and students. The real question then is, "do you think that colleges and universities should stop doing these horrible things?" and of course anyone who understands it that way (and what other way is there to understand it?) will answer "yes" and thus provide Boehner and McKeon with one more piece of "evidence" with which to convict higher education of multiple offenses.

If a question doesn't coerce, it imputes blame where there may not be any. Here is question 12: "Do you believe the construction of facilities at colleges and universities is contributing to the dramatic increases in the cost of higher education?" The suggestion is that a "yes" answer (to which the respondent is obviously directed) would mean that colleges and universities were doing something wrong. But what would it be? Constructing laboratories? dormitories? libraries? classroom buildings? Could an academic institution be doing its job and *not* be constructing facilities? What's the point of this question? No point really, accept to add one more (underdefined) item to the list of crimes of which colleges and universities are presumed guilty in this indictment masquerading as a survey.

It is not an indictment solely constructed by Boehner and McKeon, who are merely playing their part in a coordinated effort to commandeer higher education by discrediting it. If the public can be persuaded that institutions of higher education are fiscally and pedagogically irresponsible, the way will be open to a double agenda: strip colleges and universities of both federal and state support and then tie whatever funds are left to "performance" measures in the name of account-ability and assessment. The folks who gave us the politi-cal correctness scare in the '90s (and that was one of the best PR campaigns ever mounted) are once again in high gear and their message is simple: higher education is too important to be left to the educators, who are wasting your money, teaching your children to be unpatriotic and irreli-gious (when they are teaching at all), and running a closed shop that is hostile to the values of mainstream America. It's a potent formula: less money, more controls, and controls by the right people; not pointy-headed professors or wooly-headed administrators, but hard-headed businessmen who will rein in the excesses (monetary and moral) to which people with too many advanced degrees are prone.

So much is clear and indisputable. What is not clear is the response of the academic community to this assault on its autonomy and professional integrity. Too often that response has been of the weak-kneed variety displayed by the Asso-ciation of American Universities when then president Nils Hasselmo offered a mild criticism of Mr. McKeon's ideas and then said, "We look forward to working with Mr. McKeon." No, you should look forward to defeating Mr. McKeon and his ilk, and that won't be done by mealymouthed me-tooism. If the academic community does its usual thing and rolls over and plays dead, in time it will *be* dead.

But what is the alternative? One step would be to edu-cate the general public, something I attempted on a small scale when I was dean and a parent, in the course of making a complaint, would say to me, "After all, as a taxpayer I pay your salary." I always responded by asking a question: what percentage of the university's operating costs do you guess are covered by public funds? Almost always, the answer was something on the order of 75 percent. When I said, no, the figure is just 25 percent and heading downward and added that in some states the figure has dipped below 10 percent, the reaction was usually one of surprise and dismay.

I followed up with another question: what percentage of the cost to educate a student do you guess is covered by tuition? Again, the parent was usually shocked by the answer: if you include not just classroom education but the cost of everything that must be in place for that education to occur—a library, laboratories, computer centers, building maintenance, utilities, safety patrols, and more—tuition covers only 26 percent. At this point in the conversation the unhappy parent began to see what public universities are facing these days: "You're telling me that state funds are being withdrawn at the same time expenses are exceeding tuition by a factor of four to one, and you're barred by law from raising tuition. How can you stay in business?"

A good question, but one more appropriately put to the people who are doing the damage, the state and federal officials who are supposedly in charge of ensuring the health and prosperity of higher education. It is they who must be made to confront the consequences of their actions.

Again, I tried to do my small part when I was a dean. In the course of several years, I said many nasty things about members of Congress, Illinois state representatives and senators, the governor of Illinois, the governor's budget director, and the governor-appointed Illinois Board of Higher Education. I called these people ignorant, misinformed, demagogic, and dishonest and repeatedly suggested that when it came to colleges and universities, either they didn't know what they were talking about or (and this is worse) they did know and were deliberately setting out to destroy public higher education.

In response they sent me nice notes, trekked across the state to visit me in my office, invited me to talk with their colleagues, bought my books (and actually read them), took me to lunch, and promised to arrange a dinner with the governor. (It never happened.)

What was going on here? Why did people of whom I had been unfailingly (and acerbically) critical respond by being unfailingly nice and even, on occasion, deferential?

I got the hint of an answer from the first state representative who came to see me. As she walked through the door, she said, "Well, I managed to find your office, so we all can't be as dumb as you say we are." Two things were obvious: she had certainly gotten the message. And it was the message—harsh, accusatory, scornful—that had gotten her to come.

The conclusion I drew from this and other interactions was not that public life is full of masochists looking for a chance to be beaten again, but that senior university administrators and lobbyists have been talking to legislators and governors (and, yes, trustees) in the wrong way.

That is, campus administrators have been diplomatic, respectful, conciliatory, reasonable, sometimes apologetic, and always defensive, and they would have done much better, I think, if they had been aggressive, blunt, mildly confrontational, and just a bit arrogant. When I talked to university officials and suggested that they go on the offensive when faced with budget cuts, threats of new control, baseless accusations of waste, etc., they demurred and said, "It wouldn't be good to irritate them."

Well, "irritate" is not quite what I had in mind. "Get their attention" is more in the right direction, "make them uncomfortable" would be better, and "cause them pain" would hit the mark. It was Ronald Reagan who figured out that a university system offers the perfect target for making political (and sometimes financial) hay because it is at once visible and populated by persons who, although (or because) they are the bearers of many advanced degrees, are unlikely to fight back. Or, if they do fight back, it will be with tools that are spectacularly ineffectual.

Those will be, not surprisingly, the tools of their trade—fact, reason, argument, theory, never anything ad hoc or ad hominem. So when, for the ten-thousandth time, the charge is made that faculty members only teach six or nine or twelve hours a week and spend the rest of their time doing pointless research or drinking lattes in a cafe, the university community will respond with mind-numbing statistics, with elaborate (and largely unpersuasive) accounts of how the state will ultimately benefit from a study of gender reversal in Shakespeare or from a mathematical proof that only five people in the world understand, and (although it doesn't follow at all) with a resolution to do better. And then next year or next month when the same things are said, it will have to be done all over again, and with as little effect.

In general, there are two things that won't work, and they are the only two things universities ever try.

First of all, it won't work to explain the academic world to nonacademics while standing on one foot. That is, you can't in a short time teach people to value activities they have never engaged in, or persuade them that if research into the ways and byways of Byzantine art is not supported, the world will be poorer. Remember, it takes four or more years to initiate students into the pleasures of the academic life, and in many cases the effort is not successful. Why should anyone think that the lessons could be taught and accepted in twenty minutes?

If telling our story in the hope that its terms will be adopted by those who have never lived it won't work, neither will the attempt to translate it into their terms by retelling it in the vocabulary of business or venture capitalism.

Colleges and universities surely must observe good business practices in the relevant areas (purchasing, service contracts, construction, maintenance), but colleges, as I have said earlier, are not businesses. They do not drop product lines that have lost market share. They do not dismiss employees who cease to be productive or run into a bad patch. They do not monitor every moment of every working day. They will wait years for a research program to pan out and won't consider it a breach of contract if it doesn't.

To be sure, sometimes a faculty project will pay off (with a patent, a large grant, a Nobel Prize), but more often it will not even pay its own way. If a bottom-line criterion is applied to the academy, 90 percent of what goes on will fail the test, and, therefore, defending the academy in bottom-line terms is a losing proposition, unless you want to reach the conclusion that most of what academics do should be abandoned.

But what's left? If explaining to our critics what we do won't work, and if redescribing the enterprise in the vocabulary of their vocations won't work either, what will work?

Well, maybe nothing. Maybe the academy will just have to learn to live (and perhaps die) in this brave new world where money is withdrawn from public higher education at the same time that ever more strict controls are imposed. But my experience suggests that it might just be worth a try to stand up for ourselves unapologetically, and to comport ourselves as if we were formidable adversaries rather than easy marks.

This would mean allowing no false statement by a public official to pass uncorrected and unrebuked. (Not only must the record be set straight; those who have gotten it wrong must be made to feel bad if only so that they will think twice before doing it again.) It would mean embracing the fact that few nonacademics understand what we do and why we do it, and turning it into a weapon. Instead of saying, "Let me tell you what we do so that you'll love us," or "Let me explain how your values are really our values too," say, "We do what we do, we've been doing it for a long time, it has its own history, and until you learn it or join it, your opinions are not worth listening to."

Instead of defending classics or French literature or sociology, ask those who think they need defending what they know about them, and if the answer is "not much" (on the model of "don't know much about the Middle Ages"), suggest, ever so politely, that they might want to go back to school. Instead of trying to justify your values (always a weak position), assume them and assume too your right to define and protect them. And when you are invited to explain, defend, or justify, just say no.

But again, will it work? It just might (I offer no guarantees), and for two reasons. First, it will be surprising, and, because surprising, disconcerting: legislators, governors, and trustees don't expect academics to hit back or (even better) hit first, and at the least you will have gotten them off balance. Second, they quite possibly will like it, will like being challenged rather than toadied to, will like being taken seriously enough to engage with, will like being party to a conversation of the kind that fills our days, will like, in short, being spoken to as if they were academics.

The attraction that bashing the academy has for politicians and others has a source in the anti-intellectualism that has always been a part of American life. It is our version of the no-nonsense empiricism and distrust of eloquence bequeathed to us by the British and refined into an art in the "a man's gotta do what a man's gotta do" spirit of Western expansion.

But that same anti-intellectualism has its flip side in an abiding fascination with those who devote themselves to what is called (I dislike the phrase, but it is sometimes useful) the life of the mind. Nonacademics either want to beat us up or have dinner with us. If we don't let them do the first—if we fight back with all we have and all we are—we'll have more chances to do the second; and a familiarity not rooted in contempt might in time pay off.

Will it happen? I doubt it. Once I found myself sitting in a doctor's waiting room, and sitting next to me was one of the university's lobbyists. We talked and commiserated about budgetary woes, new demands and restrictions, recycled misconceptions, and the like. As one of us (I forgot which) got called into the inner sanctum, I said, "The next time you go before some committee in the legislature, take me with you." He said, "Will you behave?"

Some people never learn.

# SEVEN

# A Conclusion and Two Voices
# from the Other Side

In conclusion, let me summarize my argument and the entailments it implies. The grounding proposition is that both the coherence and the value of a task depend on its being distinctive. Beginning with that proposition, I ask: What is the distinctive task college and university professors are trained and paid to perform? What can they legitimately (as opposed to presumptuously) claim to be able to do? My answer is that college and university professors can introduce students to bodies of material new to them and equip those same students with the appropriate (to the discipline) analytical and research skills. From this professional competence follow both obligations and prohibitions. The obligations are the usual pedagogical ones—setting up a course, preparing a syllabus, devising exams, assigning papers or experiments, giving feedback, holding office hours, etc. The prohibitions are that an instructor should do neither less nor more.

Doing less would mean not showing up to class or showing up unprepared, not being alert to the newest approaches and models in the field, failing to give back papers or to comment on them in helpful ways, etc. Doing more would be to take on tasks that belong properly to other agents—to preachers, political leaders, therapists, and gurus. The lure of these other (some would say larger or more noble) tasks is that they enhance, or at least seem to enhance, the significance of what a teacher does. But in fact, I argue, agendas imported into the classroom from foreign venues do not enrich the pedagogical task, but overwhelm it and erode its constitutive distinctiveness. Once you start preaching or urging a political agenda or engaging your students in discussions designed to produce action in the world, you are surely doing something, but it is not academic, even if you give it that name.

You know you are being academic (rather than therapeutic or political or hortatory) when the questions raised in your classroom have the goal of achieving a more accurate description or of testing a thesis; you know that you are being (or trying to be) something else when the descriptions you put forward are really stepping stones to an ideological conclusion (even one so apparently innocuous as "we should respect the voices of others"). The academic enterprise excludes no topic from its purview, but it regards any and every topic as a basis for analysis rather than as a stimulus to some moral, political, or existential commitment. Not to practice politics, but to study it; not to proselytize for or against religious doctrines, but to describe them; not to affirm or reject affirmative action, but to explore its history and lay out the arguments that have been made for and against it.

My contention is that if every college or university instructor were to hew to this discipline—were to do his or her job and refrain from doing jobs that belong appropriately to others—those who want to do our jobs for us would have no traction or point of polemical entry because politics, or religion, or ethics would enter the classroom only as objects of analysis and not as candidates for approval or rejection. The culture wars, at least in the classroom, would be over. There would still be a basis for argument and correction. You could still say, I don't think your account is quite right for the following reasons. But the reasons would belong to the canons of argument and evidence and not to any political, religious, or ethical agenda.

The name I give to this academic categorical imperative is "academicizing." To academicize an issue is to detach it from those contexts where it poses a choice of what to do or how to live—shall I join the priesthood or join the army?—and insert it into an academic context where it invites a certain kind of interrogation. What is its history? Why has it been thought significant? What are the prevailing answers to the questions it raises? Where do those answers come from? The more these and related questions are posed, the less will students feel the urgency to bear personal witness in one direction or another.

But for many, that is just the problem. I acknowledged at the outset that mine is a minority position. Indeed, in some quarters it is a position regarded as so neolithic and retrograde that no one bothers even to argue against it. Mark Bracher, a professor at Kent State, begins a recent essay by declaring confidently, "Many literature teachers and scholars are committed to promoting social justice through both their teaching and their scholarship." Bracher spends no time discussing whether promoting social justice is an appropriate academic goal. He is just distressed that not very much has been done in the way of accomplishing it. "But despite this commitment of critical and pedagogical activity to political and ethical ends, there is little evidence that literary study has made much difference in the injustice that permeates our world." (To me, that's the good news.)

Injustice would be diminished, Bracher believes, if sympathy and compassion for others were increased. And that, he says, should be the work of the classroom: "If literary study could systematically help students overcome their indifference to the suffering that surrounds them, and experience compassion for the sufferers, it would make a significant contribution to social justice." But literary study could have this effect only if it were no longer literary study, that is, if the study of stylistic effects, genres, meters, verse forms, novels, romance, epic, the contest of interpretations—everything that belongs to literary study as something distinctive, something one could master, something one could teach—were made instrumental to an end not contemplated by those who either produce the literature or consume it. To be sure, some poets or novelists write with the purpose of expanding the sympathies of their readers, but what of those who do not? Either their works will be distorted when they are bent to a measure foreign to their intention, or they will not be taught because they are not useful to the *nonliterary* purpose of the course. Either way, the course will be a course in literary study only by name, and the students will be offered a character transplant when they signed on for something more modest, to wit, a course of instruction.

But who gave Mark Bracher (or any other teacher employed by a college or university) the authority first to decide what the world and his students need in the way of moral improvement, and second to turn his classroom into a social/ethical laboratory? Isn't that straight indoctrination? Bracher asks the same questions and answers that the objection is naïve because indoctrination is already occurring anyway. "As currently practiced, literary pedagogy . . . contributes to the production of docile subjects for global capitalism through, for example, enforcing classroom punctuality, reliability, obedience, and subordination." The account of cause and effect here is more than a bit crude. Is it really the case that if you come to class, and, even worse, come to class on time, and, worse still, conform your behavior to the protocols of classroom discipline, you will become a capitalist toady? (If only the work of ideology were that easy.) But the specific example Bracher offers is less important than his general argument that because there is no avoiding imposing values in one direction or another, we might as well impose the values in the direction we prefer: "we should forthrightly acknowledge that it is our job to change our students' behaviors and turn our attention to the question of what behaviors we should try to change, and what means we should use to do so." In short, if we don't push our politics, the classroom will be taken over by someone else's. After all, isn't everything political?

I have addressed this question several times in the course of this book, but it cannot be answered too often, if only because the "everything-is-political" mantra is ritually invoked by those who do not respect (or believe in) the distinction between academic work and political work. If by "political" we mean the presence in a situation of competing visions of the good and the true, then of course everything is political, for no form of socially organized life—be it marriage, industry, church life, the military, in addition to politics per se—is free of ideological conflict, and even when conflicts are (temporarily) resolved, the shape of the resolution will at some level be political too. But the fact that politics marks every context of human action doesn't mean that it is legitimate to import the politics appropriate to one context into another which, while no less political, will be home to a quite different politics There are corporate politics, domestic politics, office politics, mail-room politics, and locker-room politics, in addition to partisan politics and academic politics, and each of these will have different contents which in turn will legitimate different forms of political behavior. (In partisan politics, ad hominem attacks are within the pale; in academic politics, they are not.)

The content of academic politics is, among other things, disagreement about what texts should be taught, what methodological approaches are legitimate, what courses should be required, and which reading of a poem is correct. The content of partisan politics is, among other things, disagreement about what alliances the country should form, which wars it should wage, what social goals it should mandate, and which party should be elected. In both arenas, the political agent is trying to persuade his or her fellows to a particular conclusion; but in one the goal of persuasion is the adoption of a policy or a change in the country's direction, while in the other the goal is to establish, by argument and evidence, the superiority of one analysis or description or procedure over its (intellectual) rivals. If I vote against a literary theorist and for a Shakespearian in a tenure meeting, my act can be described as political because I am aligning myself with one party rather than another in an academic debate about personnel and curriculum. If I vote for a candidate or donate money to a cause, my action is also political, but in an entirely different register. I am trying to change the world rather than to change the minds of my colleagues about the future direction of the discipline.

It may seem paradoxical to say so, but the truth of the assertion that the political is everywhere means that there is no overarching sense of the political, no politics that is just politics per se, no politics that seeps into everything; there are just particular instances of politics in particular conventional/social settings. "Everything is political" means that there is no situation free of political contestation, not that the form of political contestation you find over here will be exactly like the form of political contestation you find over there. Correctly understood, the "everything is political" slogan sends you back to the differences—between practices and disciplines—those who invoke it want to deny. Once you realize that while politics is everywhere, it isn't the same politics, the cash value of saying that everything is political disappears; for it won't get those who say it to where they want to get—to a justification for bringing the politics appropriate to one project (the project of trying to elect people or pass laws) into the precincts of another (the project of determining which account of an academic matter is correct). That justification would only be available if there were a general category of the political apart from any particular contexts of political action, if all politics were the same in a stronger sense than the sense given by the lexical fact that they can be referred to by the same word. The availability of the word "political" to refer to what goes on in different contexts is what tricks people into thinking that the boundaries between contexts are illusory and without constraining or distinguishing effect.

It is only because he believes in the chimera of a general politics filling all nooks and crannies that Bracher can think he's scored a point when he asks, "Don't we choose our texts, formulate our writing assignments and organize classroom activities with the aim of getting our students to respond in particular ways?" Isn't that political? Yes, we do, and yes it is, but if we are teaching rather than proselytizing—doing academic politics and not ballot box politics—the particular responses we hope to elicit are responses to an academic question (what is the structure of this argument? is this text unified? is this account of the event complete?) and not to the question of what we should do about the economy or the AIDS epidemic or the pollution of the environment. Bracher needs to conflate those questions so that he can pursue his partisan agenda with a good conscience, so that he can say that because everything is political (a claim that is both true and trivial), we teachers can do anything we like.

At one point Bracher claims—it is an incredible claim—that his agenda is "politically neutral" and "aims not to inculcate particular values" but to "provide students with more complete, empirically and clinically validated knowledge of the causes of certain behaviors" he finds distressing. But within two paragraphs, he identifies these malign causes with the "American ideology that emphasizes hyper-individualism, self-reliance and social Darwinism"; within a few sentences "American ideology" has become "conservative ideology"; and within a few pages George W. Bush has emerged as an example of the conservative thinking that teachers must expose and oppose. Later Bush appears in a list with Osama bin Laden and Saddam Hussein as figures "toward whom [students] may feel animosity" of the kind they certainly feel toward "murderers, rapists, child molesters, and other criminals." If this is political neutrality, I wonder what political advocacy looks like.

Bracher is self-aware enough to ask the obvious question: "what right do we have to impose our view . . .—our 'liberal' or 'progressive' ideology—on our students?" "We have the right," he answers, "because the evidence supports . . . our ideology." In short, we're correct, those other guys are on the wrong side, and while we don't want them turning students into apologists for global capitalism, it's perfectly okay—indeed obligatory and moral—for us to turn students into agents of left-progressive change. Any conservative parent, legislator, or donor reading Bracher's essay will have plenty of evidence to support the conviction that liberal professors have abandoned teaching for indoctrination. Of course for Bracher this would not be an accusation. In his view teaching *is* indoctrination and the only question is, will it be our indoctrination or theirs?

The desire to indoctrinate is not the only reason some will reject the imperative always to academicize. There is also the desire to inspire, to bring one's students not simply to a point of understanding a subject matter but to a level of moral illumination that will infuse every moment of their lives with a deep meaning. In a recent book subtitled *Why Our Colleges and Universities Have Given Up on the Meaning of Life*, Anthony Kronman complains that an "old idea that a program of higher education should be . . . organized around the questions of the ends of human life lost its appeal in favor of a new idea that a college or a university is . . . a gathering of academic specialists inspired by their commitment to scholarship as a vocation." The old idea, the idea of providing training in the general "art of living," placed no bounds on the ambitions of a teacher who wanted to lead students in a search for the meaning of life. The new idea, the idea of teachers and students joined in an effort to determine the truth of a disciplinary matter—the interpretation of a poem, the causes of an event, the origins of a virus—limits both the kinds of questions that can be asked and the answers that can be appropriately given. Kronman would have us break out of these limits ("What is needed is relief from the inhibitions of the research ideal"), but it is my view that those very limits, if they are honored, allow us to identify with precision the tasks we are equipped to perform—teach materials and confer skills—and protect us from the accusation that we have ventured into precincts (of politics, morality, ethics) not properly ours.

The promise Kronman holds out is glorious. Teachers and students who are put in touch with the deep and abiding concerns that animate the great works of literature, philosophy, and history might experience a "kind of immortality" and even enact "the idea of eternity in their lives." No such reward awaits the disciplinary worker who must be satisfied with particulars and the narrow goal of making an account, or a description, or an interpretation just a bit more adequate to its object. Nevertheless, I maintain, it is the very modesty of the academicizing enterprise—its forsaking of the grand vision to which Kronman would call us—that makes it coherent and intelligible.

When Kronman links education to the search for an answer to "the question of life's meaning," he enrolls himself in a venerable humanistic tradition that includes, among others, Cicero, John Milton, Philip Sidney, Matthew Arnold. This is an impressive list that could easily be enlarged tenfold, but I have my own roster of worthies to invoke. "It is absolutely essential," declares Kant, "that the learned community at the university... contain a faculty that is independent... one that having no commands to give, is free to evaluate everything." Cardinal Newman says the same thing in a formulation that anticipates everything I have written here: "The process of training, by which the intellect, instead of being formed or sacrificed to some particular or accidental purpose, some specific trade or profession... is disciplined for its own sake... is called Liberal Education." And Jacques Derrida provides a deeply philosophical justification of the austerity I have been urging. "Thinking, if it is to remain open to the possibility of thought... must not seek to be economic." That is, it must not rest on the hope of a "real world" payoff. Why? Because "it belongs... to an economy of waste," an economy whose currency purchases nothing beyond its own expenditure. Therefore, Derrida concludes,

"Beware of ends." Beware, that is, of doing something for a reward external to its own economy. Do it because it is its own reward and look for no pleasures beyond the pleasure of responsible, rigorous performance. In short, and for the last time, just do your job. The world of grand and ambitious ends will take care of itself, and if it doesn't, you can always save it on your own time.

# Selected Bibliography

Academic Bill of Rights. Available at studentsforacademicfreedom.org.

Althouse, Ann. "Stanley Fish Takes on the Kevin Barret Controversy." Available at http://www.althouse.blogspot.com/2006/07/stanley-fish-takes-on-kevin-barrett.html.

American Association of University Professor's 1915 Declaration of Principles. Available at http://www.akronaaup.org/documents/AAUP1915.pdf.

Bennett, William. *Why We Fight: Moral Clarity and the War on Terrorism*. New York: Doubleday, 2002.

Boehner, John A., and Howard McKeon. "College Cost Crisis." Available at http://www.epi.elps.vt.edu/Perspectives/collegecostsrep.pdf.

Bok, Derek. *Our Underachieving Colleges*. Princeton, N.J.: Princeton University Press, 2006.

Bracher, Mark. "Teaching for Social Justice: Reeducating the Emotions through Literary Study." *JAC* 26 (2006): 464.

Carey, John. "A Work in Praise of Terrorism? September 11 and *Samson Agonistes*." *Times Literary Supplement*, 6 Sept. 2002: 15–16.

Churchill, Ward. "The Ghosts of 9-1-1: Reflections on History, Justice and Roosting Chickens." Available at http://www.altpr.org.

Churchill, Ward. "'Some People Push Back': On the Justice of Roosting Chickens." Available at http://www.ratical.org.

Cottom, Daniel. *Why Education Is Useless*. Philadelphia: University of Pennsylvania Press, 2003.

Dennison, George M. "State Funding Leads toward Privatization." Available at http://www.umt.edu/urelations/MainHall/1102/funding.htm.

Dworkin, Ronald. "Liberalism." In *Public and Private Morality*, edited by Stuart Hampshire. New York: Cambridge University Press, 1978.

Gearen, Mark D. Letter to the *New York Times*, 24 May 2004.

Gerber, Larry. "Inextricably Linked: Shared Governance and Academic Freedom." *Academe* 87 (May–June 2001): 22–24.

Graff, Gerald. *Beyond the Culture Wars*. New York: W. W. Norton & Company, 1992.

Haynsworth, Harry J. "Faculty Governance: Reflections of a Retiring Dean." *University of Toledo Law Review* (fall 2003): 93–100.

Hinshaw, Wendy Wolters. "Teaching for Social Justice? Resituating Student Resistance." *JAC* 27 (2007): 222–34.

Horowitz, David. "The Campus Blacklist." Available at http://www.frontpagemag.com/articles/Read.aspx?GUID=18DCCD2C-275B-489E-B920-266043279A09.

*Indoctrinate U*. DVD. Directed by Evan Coyne Maloney. 2007.

Kant, Immanuel. "The Contest of Faculties." In *Kant: Political Writings*, edited by H. S. Reiss. Cambridge: Cambridge University Press, 1991.

Kaplinsky, Joe. "Creationism, Pluralism, and the Compromising of Science." *Spiked*, 1 March 2005. Available at http://www.spiked-online.com/Articles/0000000CA910.htm.

Keller, Julia. "After the Attack, Postmodernism Loses Its Glib Grip." *Chicago Tribune*, 27 Sept. 2001.

Kiss, Elizabeth, and Peter Euben, eds. *Debating Moral Education*. Durham, N.C.: Duke University Press, 2008.

Kronman, Anthony. *Education's End: Why Our Colleges and Universities Have Given Up on the Meaning of Life*. Binghamton, N.Y.: Vail-Ballou Press, 2007.

Lipstadt, Deborah. *Denying the Holocaust*. New York: Penguin Group, 1994.

Locke, John. *A Letter Concerning Toleration*, edited by John Horton and Susan Mendus. New York: Routledge, 1991.

Locke, Robert. "The Liberal University: Our Demands." Available at http://www.frontpagemag.com/Articles/Read.aspx?GUID=5630FDCD-32B9-4BB1-A01D-2C39006389CB.

Leo, John. "Campus Hand-Wringing Is Not a Pretty Sight." Available at http://www.johnleo.com.

Lombardi, John V. "University Improvement: The Permanent Challenge." Available at http://www.jvlone.com.

McGrory, Brian. "Chill Sets In at Harvard." *Boston Globe*, 21 Jan. 2005. Available at http://www.boston.com/news/local/articles/2005/01/21/chill_sets_in_at_harvard.

Mearsheimer, John. "The Aims of Education." *Philosophy and Literature* 22 (1998): 137–55.

Michigan State University Mission Statement. Available at http://president.msu.edu/mission.php.

Mill, John Stuart. *On Liberty*. New York: Penguin Books, 1974.

Murphy, James Bernard. "Good Students and Good Citizens." *New York Times*, 15 Sept. 2002.

Nagel, Thomas. "Moral Conflict and Political Legitimacy." *Philosophy and Public Affairs* 16 (1987): 215–40.

Neal, Anne. "Intellectual Diversity Endangered." Available at http://www.cfif.org/htdocs/freedomline/current/guest_commentary/student_right_to_learn.htm.

Newman, John Henry. *The Idea of a University*. London: Longmans, Green and Co., 1893.

Rothstein, Edward. "Attacks on U.S. Challenge the Perspectives of Postmodern True Believers." *New York Times*, 22 Sept. 2001, late edition, A17.

Selingo, Jeffrey. "The Disappearing State in Public Higher Education." *Chronicle of Higher Education* 49 (2003).

Street, Paul. "A Farewell Message from Stanley Fish: 'Good Professors Do What They're Told.'" Available at http://www.punksinscience.org.

Taylor, Mark. *The Moment of Complexity*. Chicago: University of Chicago Press, 2001.

*United States v. Philip Morris*. United States District Court for the District of Columbia, Civil Action No. 99–2496 (GK), 2006.

University of Arizona Guidelines for Shared Governance. Available at http://w3fp.arizona.edu/senate/ShGovExtending.html.

Waldron, Jeremy. "What Plato Would Allow?" *Nomos* XXXVII, 1995.

Weinrib, Ernest J. "Legal Formalism: On the Immanent Rationality of Law." *Yale Law Journal* 97 (1988).

Weslyan University Mission Statement. Available at http://www.wesleyan.edu/deans/mission.html.

Yale College Mission Statement. Available at http://www.yale.edu/accred/standards/s1.html.

Yudof, Mark. "Point of View: Is the Public Research University Dead?" *Chronicle of Higher Education*, 11 Jan. 2002.

# Index

Made in the USA
Lexington, KY
10 December 2014